The Art of Serving with Happiness

Leadership and success in the art of serving

JESÚS NEIRA QUINTERO

snow
fountain
press

THE ART OF SERVING WITH HAPPINESS
Jesús Neira Quintero, 2021
© First Edition in Spanich, 2017
All rights reserved.

Snow Fountain Press
25 SE 2nd. Avenue, Suite 316
Miami, FL 33131
www.snowfountainpress.com

ISBN: 978-1-951484-82-8

Editorial diagramming and design:
Alynor Diaz

Traslated by:
Silvia Rafti

Printed in the United States of America.

EVERYTHING YOU SHOULD KNOW ABOUT LEADERSHIP AND THE ART OF SERVING WITH HAPPINESS.

The approaches set out in this book are intended to
resolve the following questions
on servant management:

What is their attitude?
Why do they fail?
What are their characteristics?
How do they project themselves?
Why do they make mistakes?

These are some of the approaches you will find in
this work. Furthermore, you will also learn about
organizational culture, the mastery of ethics, and the
essential elements for
whoever wants to be a good servant and a great leader
and enjoy his craft or profession with happiness.

INDEX

- Prologue 9
- The Art of Serving with Happiness 11
- Introduction 15

CHAPTER I 21
- The servant and his integrity 21
- The patient servant 25
- The purposeful servant 28
- The scattered servant 30
- The friendly servant 32
- The dispute over the word 34
- How to avoid war over the right to speak 36
- How to conduct your tasks with discipline? 38

CHAPTER II 41
- The authenticity of the servant
- The servant who believes to own the truth 43
- The servant who abuses his role 45

CHAPTER III 49
- Wisdom and sensibility in the art of serving
- Human rights and the servant 49
- The servant that enjoys the pain of others 51
- The attitude of the offended servant 52
- The servant and his self-esteem 52
- The servant with class 54
- The servant that never loses 55
- The angry servant 57
- The servant that enjoys his work activity 59
- The tardy servant 61
- The honest servant 62

- The organized servant 63
- The servant who uses critical thinking 64
- The dissociating servant 65
- The arrogant servant 66
- The servant with a desire to improve 69
- The evasive servant 72
- The creative servant 73
- The servant with a sense of service 76
- Sincerity, the quality that enhances service 78
- The servant who does not complicate simplicity 80
- The prudent servant 82
- The servant with good manners 83
- The servant that manages his time 85
- The simulating servant 87
- The loyal servant 87
- The visionary servant 89
- The nonconformist servant 90

CHAPTER IV 93
• **Leadership and the servant**
- Why do servants fail? 98

CHAPTER V 101
• **The servant's ethics and values**
- Ethical values of the good servant 101
- The servant's behavior 105
- Corruption 105

CHAPTER VI 107

• **The emotionally ill servant**

- Anxiety and the servant 108

- How to manage stress 112

- How to create a stress-free company 115

- The servant and his emotional quotient 117

Bibliography 118

PROLOGUE

Human beings, regardless of age and culture, face change as a constant process, and therefore, we are obliged to assimilate many factors that affect the way we live. And even if many things change, our fundamental needs remain the same, so our mission is to provide ourselves with a full life, growth, and happiness.

Each generation has had to navigate the avatars of their history while leaving a tangible and spiritual legacy where the progressive illusion of tomorrow is preserved. This continuous sowing is possible because we are aware of the transcendence of our actions, and beyond material urgency lies the human will to think of the other, of their well-being. This virtue, which is the attitude, delimits the result of who we are and what we do.

Perhaps some people among us would instead move away from the world of human beings and enter the depths of a forest or live in the unattainable peak of a mountain to not have to deal with other beings of their species. Unsociable characters do not exist only in novels, and an overdose of bitterness may have the power to turn a tender rose into the fiercest of thorns. It is not necessary to get to extremes. It is here that a book like *The Art of Serving with Happiness* illuminates a universal setting because to survive, each of us must provide something or serve someone, literally. And that something is life and that someone, in the first instance, is oneself.

Fortunately, we humans also have the ability to renew ourselves, as the universe does, and if that process of transformation is for the sake of happiness: Eureka! But desiring to be happy is not enough; you have to know how to be happy, especially regarding personal expectations, coexistence, and workplace demands.

It is inconceivable to think of a world of independent relationships when reality operates as an interdependent matrix that impacts everything and everyone, so let us ignore the backgrounds of its scope. Let us think of a society that, along with its fundamental needs, must meet those of self-realization, self-esteem, social interaction, security, and physiological needs, as the psychologist Abraham Maslow put it. It requires a social synergy that allows each individual to meet their needs and for this chain of well-being to radiate peace and harmony exponentially, so the system does not weaken and collapse. When a link in this chain breaks, it is because this synergy has not been achieved. Serving with happiness is a serious topic for its implications. Personal and professional growth is what writer Jesús Neira Quintero, an institution on public and private service, presents through his experience and research.

The Art of Serving with Happiness is a call to individual reflection to learn to recognize our weaknesses, develop new behaviors, and overcome one or more of the categories that the illustrious man of laws has defined in analyzing the act of serving from different perspectives. Likewise, it is a call to companies, whether public or private, to invest in happiness as an organizational goal that is undoubtedly one of the best indicators of growth of any entrepreneurship. Serving is a vital exercise in existence and should not be tarnished by stigmas or behaviors that can be easily corrected, as the author teaches in this work. A happy being radiates harmony in everything he does, keeps his values high, and creates opportunities for all.

Serving is an art, and those who master the art of serving with happiness and excellence hold in their hands the key to success.

Pilar Velez
Writer, collaborating member American Academy
of the Spanish Language (ANLE)

The Art of Serving with Happiness

Friendly reader:

The book that the publisher puts in your hands today is a small gem of contemporary literature. Its author, writer Jesús Neira Quintero, is responsible for analyzing one of the activities that, within human behavior, has an extraordinary conceptual value: service. That is, the way each human being adjusts their social behavior most productively and generously that our nature can conceive in the act of providing help to those who need it, in an attempt to make that person happy.

I had the pleasant opportunity to be a guest professor at Tamkang University (Graduate Institute of Latin American Studies) in the Republic of China, ROC, in 1991. During this teaching experience, I captured with curious attention how the society of that great country professes and bears a special reverence for the culture of service to others. In an even more surprising way, I noticed the admiration and respect offered to the figure of the servant. Indeed, Taoism teaches, "Whoever wants to be served must serve others first." Similarly, in Judeo-Christian culture, there are repeated and beautiful expressions of the same precepts.

Years later, I found in treatise writer Jesus Neira Quintero, a distinguished academic and law specialist, a writer who brilliantly and judiciously wrote a complete and detailed essay on the service of public officials in Colombia, an obligatory consultation reference for the Hispanic legal world. That book is titled *The Good Public Servant*.

Today, Professor Neira Quintero has successfully expanded the content of his original work to offer audiences in the United States this new book.

I welcome his wonderful initiative since, in this publication, he explains and further expands the projection of his fruitful thinking in dealing with the philosophy of service for the sake of our fellowmen. Indeed, the great Mahatma Gandhi teaches that "... the best way to find yourself is to lose yourself in the service of others."

I cannot resist the temptation to mention another beautiful passage by R. Tagore, "I slept and dreamed that life was joy. I woke up and saw that life was service. I served and saw that life was happiness."

The scholarly author of *The Art of Serving with Happiness* impacts readers with profound and accurate quotes from historical characters until obtaining, as he has done, a brief and helpful manual of ethics, principles, and values that borders the best books of self-improvement and spiritual growth published in the United States.

Some will wonder what the merit of this beautiful compendium is. I think that writer Neira Quintero has understood and developed, better than other authors, the greatness of humility and the secret of happiness in the apostolate of service.

It is not strange for this Colombian thinker to have developed such refined and original ideas about the art of serving, since his own life has been a continuous experience of service to his fellow citizens as a lawyer, public official, teacher, educator, counselor, and also a consummate musician. Undoubtedly, the reason for his successful career as a writer lies in condensing in his writings the virtues that lead directly to happiness, hidden in one of the simplest, and, at the same time, noble acts in the daily life of every human being: to serve others, show solidarity and help those who need it, regardless of the nature of the service, without distinction of hierarchy or performance and the expectation of any remuneration.

The president of a state is as much a servant as the worker repairing shoes in his humble workshop.

Throughout these pages, the reader must find a tally of wise precepts and values that, when inviting reflection, lead to the quietness and disposition of spirit, necessary to rescue joy, not infrequently sequestered by the bad news of day by day, and the uncertainty of these difficult times.

This fun and useful work of training and personal growth will undoubtedly help the reader to acquire a more definite knowledge of human coexistence and good work, the ultimate goal of ethics, as the right way to find inner peace and find happiness.

Luis Carlos Fallon Borda
Colombian writer and lawyer Professor
of OLLI - University of Miami

INTRODUCTION

The Art of Serving with Happiness

Leadership and success in the art of serving

The best master key for service providers to be happier in society and reach their long-for progress is to serve with happiness. To achieve that goal, it is necessary to establish a constant desire for service and let this principle be their best ally. This produces a continuous and deep relationship with their human condition and cultivates their will for service, consisting of a permanent exercise with their moral code.

Being solidary with others is a quality of the human being; happiness in service is a personal decision that begins by consistently serving when walking the path of transparency and with a sense of purpose. Choosing to be happy when providing a good service is the best decision.

Some servants achieve happiness when their pay increases, while for others, their emotional wages are more satisfactory when engaging with others in participatory activities that bring them personal satisfaction. Being collaborative, creative, and having a vocation for service is your best reference to be happy.

It is natural for a servant's state of happiness to influence productivity. A dissenting servant does not perform the same as a worker under different conditions. A servant that cares about thinking of the other, meeting the user's needs, without being focused on the material, is happier.

A company's success depends on the happiness it can provide its workers. It should bring them more joy, not only through wage increases but also by giving them comfort in environmental, locative, recreational, and growth seminars that encourage interpersonal relationships and personal development improvement. Money is not the determining factor, but it contributes to reaching other achievements that provide happiness. This reference is not everything; often, happiness is not serving for the sake of serving, but knowing how to serve provides greater well-being within.

I quote the philosopher and writer Emilio Galán about the relationship between service and happiness:

Learn to serve with happiness

Leadership and success in the art of serving Amicus Plato, sed magis amica veritas

By a strange association of ideas when outlining the phrases of these pages, it came to mind the inhumane condition of the slave of preterit times, although sometimes we see with bewilderment how history repeats itself in our times, even under the masquerade of democratic systems... But that era of the slave, time of lashes, hunger, and disease... Ah, life...

What did those brutally enslaved creatures do to face the pain? Sing! Yes! Singing, singing, and dancing slowly, parsimoniously... It was their dance to the rhythm of scolding voices, whose tone gave away sadness, but the work progressed as a result of self-sacrifice. They thus gave value to adversity, to the cruel existence a kind smile extolling the concept of work enriching some, but exalting the prodigals in kindness and even lavishing a smile on those who afflicted them. Then, all cheerful, civilization was advancing.

I believe that this was the heritage of the overcoming of man in the face of misfortune, giving joy to the joy that comes with joy. With this, we justified the subtitle: "Leadership and success in the art of serving," but to greater abundance, the intrinsic value of truth in human existence was sought. Our flimsy ideas are soothed by the science of law that shouts to us: "Amicus Plato, sed magis amica veritas- Friend of Plato, but much more friend of the truth." Happiness makes the one who serves joyfully happy, while Truth is the vase that gathers the joy of good service.

To serve with happiness is to create relationships in genuine joy, but above all, authentic. St Francis of Assisi, the most human and most divine saint who has lived among us, bequeathed us the following lesson, "Lord, may I not so much seek to be served as to serve; to be loved, as to love; for it is in giving that we receive; it is in loving that we are loved."

Happiness is a personal decision, and if used with grace, it is the best bridge to serve. It is also necessary to develop strategies that incentivize the love of service to be more productive, effective, and become a successful servant.

My best recommendation in learning to serve with happiness is managing any vicissitude or difficulty that may arise and control emotions with a balanced mind, always with the seal of joy in service. Solidarity promotes physical and emotional health and improves the quality of life; therefore, it is essential to be affable in the workplace. This increases the value of work and enhances the work environment and interpersonal relationships with colleagues, which results in a better service. It is the degree of commitment you feel to your fellow citizens, without resentment or selfishness.

This condition is tough to achieve, for it requires enormous willpower and, many times, true renunciations. Emilio Galán expresses it in his work AXIOLOGICAL PHILOSOPHY OF THE LAW as a Latin maxim: *Ea est conditio himen, nemo sit contentus sortem suanm* (such is the condition of the man who is never happy with his luck). That is the degree of commitment.

A servant who is aware of his obligations thinks more about giving than receiving, but the slightest compensation will make him immensely happy. It is easy, then, to infer that a happy servant generates trust, and his kindness is a fundamental requirement for good coexistence. Therefore, a servant who becomes aware and nurtures his values will understand that life is too short a journey and that it makes us reflect too late.

I wish to conclude by inviting the servant to lay the foundations of his work on values. Welcome to this journey of a happy reflection in your work activity.

I hope that these reflections will help you become aware of your service role, understand others, and adopt a harmonious attitude to grow happy in the service you provide. In this sense, I want to show you the way and open your mind towards building a better service, with an attitude of change taken responsibly. A continuous exercise of principles and values is your best card to humanize this aspect, giving you happiness and developing your talents.

"Success is getting what you want. Happiness,
in enjoying what you get."
Ralph Waldo Emerson
American essayist, lecturer, philosopher, and poet

Jesús Neira Quintero

"Every day I need fewer things,
and the few things I need,
I need them very little."

St. Francis of Assisi

CHAPTER I

The servant's challenge

The servant and his integrity

*"Manage the state as you lead a family, with
authority, competence, and good example."*

Confucius
Chinese philosopher and politician

Regardless of his work activity, a good servant has to live in integrity as his primary commitment. A servant with a sense of work gives importance to his mission in every action. The servant who is the driving force of coexistence knows how to live in it; he is prepared to foster respect, trust, and solidarity; transcends in service to the community, and awakens his real influence to sow harmony and peace. A servant that acts as dean of the promotion of coexistence further enhances his service.

Pope Francis said on his visit to Ecuador that "The family constitutes the best 'social capital'; other institutions cannot replace it. It needs to be helped and strengthened, lest we lose our proper sense of the services that society as a whole provides." Furthermore, he added that those are not alms but a social debt to the family institution, which brings so much to the common good of all. A servant with a sense of family is a better person, a better client, and a mission example as a servant.

*"Courage is a desirable good that perfects the person who freely
expresses it in his behavior."*
Jorge Yarce
**International speaker of leadership,
ethics, and values.**

When there is no recognition of dignity, its meaning is stigmatized, and tolerance disappears. It is precisely in these cases when the servant must act as a teacher, leading the trust of his peers, to awaken principles of loyalty and transparency. The authentic promoter of integrity transcends service and generates spaces of harmony and well-being. To this end, he must protect the dignity of the human being, so its value is not unknown. Those who promote coexistence impose their seal of inclusion, motivate the sense of listening and the principles of legality, integrity, responsibility, transparency, loyalty, trust, respect, and other constituent values of the true servant.

The worker who has the sense of the common good clearly defined fulfills himself as a person and is able to provide an effective service with commitment, friendliness, and cooperation. Humanizing his messages rationally, emotionally, and inspiring harmony is his best investment. Find your voice and be authentic to lead within fraternity.

> *"If you can't explain it simply,*
> *you don't understand it well enough."*
> ***Albert Einstein***
> Theoretical physicist

Communicating harmony is an art that must be cultivated from within the family because it constitutes the best school of values for education and integral development. Neglect in assertive communication within the family leads to underestimating consensus.

In this age of postmodernity, when we live unfortunate situations, scholars argue that "there are times when we feel that we lose control of our emotions. Affective, labor, economic issues, and the demands and pace of daily life overwhelm us." Therefore, they recommend four simple steps to clarify the mind, reassure us, and prevent the consequences of situations that may affect coexistence and sometimes even the body:

1.Stop. Interrupt for a moment what you are doing, and stop the continuous flow of negative thoughts around that situation.

2.Breathe. Take a deep breath, feel your abdomen expand, and then exhale, allowing negative emotions to leave the body.

3.Reflect. Consider what is going on. Is it a crisis? If so, will worrying and stressing help solve it? If not, is there anything you can do and you are not doing?

4.Choose. Consider that you have options to get started. You can choose how to react to a situation; this will make you realize that you are in control of your emotions. It is here precisely where the servant must find harmony within himself to provide the service that the community requires.

As a comprehensive servant, you should consider these simple steps when dealing with complex situations that affect the community.

> *"Suit the action to the word,*
> *the word to the action."*
> **William Shakespeare**
> English playwright

A servant that makes the most of his strengths performs acts of friendliness towards others and strives to be committed, always with discipline. The servant who transmits his deepest values contributes to better treatment for peaceful living and develops his personal and business projects selflessly. A servant generating spaces of good coexistence is more productive and successful in his work. Being flexible makes him a leader without losing his beacon or route. A resilient servant wins in community, socially, business, even self-esteem.

Sonja Lyubomirsky, an American psychologist, notes that "the three main elements that really make a person happy are making friends and cultivating interpersonal relationships, learning new things or involving a challenge, and performing acts of kindness or helping others." A servant that promotes coexistence awakens and coherently exercises the sense of help for those who require the service.

More and more studies show the advantages of good humor in people's lives. Seeking opportunities to enjoy small things, not giving so much significance to everyday issues, enjoying the humor of others, and seeking the funny and kind side of life is essential, without losing your sense of responsibility and mission in the face of service. "Joy is a state that creates an emotional environment that stimulates the search for closeness." Servants that share pleasant moments manage to maintain a positive attitude in any situation and constructively face the inconveniences in their collective activity.

Live to serve and reach your fulfillment!

The patience of the servant

"It's easier to get what you want with a smile than with the tip of the sword."

William Shakespeare

Lack of patience is the basis of the poor service provided by some servants, and customers suffer it every day. The absence of this principle significantly injures the user's needs, even in events of little importance. The servant loses patience in everyday tasks in the face of the eagerness or the easiness with which he wants to develop his activity. Today's world promotes speed, immediacy, and agility to get quick results, making patience a significant challenge.

The underlying problem is a hectic lifestyle that, most of the time, leads to altered moods. Unable to stop, impulsive reactions occur that often turn into aggressive expressions. Serenity is welcome in this context, a life skill that helps us control and better manage our emotions. Serenity is an essential resource for the servant during difficult times in his environment, regardless of the vicissitudes he may be facing in his daily activity. Thus, knowing how to direct emotions leads to understanding, allowing the work to be developed patiently. Learning the intricate art of quieting the mind will enable you to have a better relationship with the user. Start by becoming aware of your work and avoid, when in a hurry, losing important facts. Try to take the time to perform your tasks and avoid performing several of them simultaneously; at the end of the day, you will surely see how you become more efficient in your job.

Another critical aspect is understanding the user's needs. They complain day after day about servants that are impatient with events of little significance. In these circumstances, wisdom is required to know how to direct your emotional quotient and put yourself in the user's place.

An impatient servant lives irritated, and the time can come when he adopts impatience as an unhealthy habit that can even affect his health. Therefore, avoid losing patience with the petty issues of everyday life. Success in handling these situations is knowing how to direct them, avoiding aggressive expressions towards the person soliciting the service, and acting calmly without being slow, which is a helpful virtue in identifying oneself as a good business leader.

> *"Suit the action to the word,*
> *the word to the action."*
> **William Shakespeare**

The current mandate to go fast is synonymous with efficiency and high capacity. Still, we forget that being impatient is countered by a productive, successful, and intelligent pace of life. My best recommendation is not to confuse patience with passivity or lack of initiative; remember that it is a skill that can be developed.

Being patient allows you to conduct your emotions with intelligence and wisdom, knowing how to direct your behavior and avoiding anxieties that often lead to adverse situations. Do not let impatience take advantage; master it, and you will see the results. If handling one's emotions skillfully is difficult, it is even more challenging to control the user's feelings. Still, a socially skilled servant tends to be a link-generating leader and a catalyst for change.

To be a servant with influence and self-confidence, you do not need to be born with emotional intelligence: you can learn from those with more experience. Remember that your emotional aptitude depends on you: your empathy generates leadership, communication, orientation to achievement, and work ethics. Also, self-mastery requires developing skills and learning to control our attitudes so that impatience does not create instability in the workplace.

A humane servant is clear about his sense of patience; he is grateful, resilient, sensitive, compassionate, positive, coherent, with a vocation for service. The above principles are his best guide to withstand whatever comes from outside and thus become the owner of exemplary behavior and empathy to transcend into assertive service to others.

A purposeful servant

*"The purpose of anthropology is to make the world safe
for human differences."*

Ruth Benedict
American anthropologist and folklorist

A good servant must be aware and recognize that he is there to serve. If you, as a servant, are clear that your mission is to fulfill your duties, you have the foundation to define how to serve well.

The first step of the servant is to polish his purpose.

Ask yourself what you are trying to accomplish with your service, why and why you do what you do and how your product or service can help create a better world. Then, by expressing your purpose in an understandable and captivating way, the user will likely react positively to it and identify with it.

A purposeful servant makes wise decisions in any situation that arises. To achieve this, engage with people who can help you achieve your goals. Do not be ashamed if you are not competent enough in some areas since accepting recommendations, guidelines, or advice greatly favors you and helps you further hone your skills to meet your goals best.

Similarly, the servant has to have goals and strategies to move forward, starting with building his brand, which will allow him to consolidate his purpose, quickly identifying his interests concerning the provision of the service.

*"Living involves having a mission; to the extent that you avoid
fighting for a valuable purpose, life will be empty."*

Jose Ortega and Gasset
Spanish philosopher and essayist

A purposeful servant multiplies all the positives in his environment and helps make it better, making his work meaningful. He is a person with a good direction in his human condition, reflecting that cluster of virtues. When, in a dehumanized way, we leave aside those we serve, we separate ourselves from our essence. In this situation, an abundant energy source is lost, which affects the quality of the work and undermines the real purpose of service.

The servant cannot allow carelessness to take over his emotions. On the contrary, he must feel that his work is worthwhile because he is at the service of others and because his actions positively impact those he serves. The servant with a real sense of purpose is inclusive, compassionate, selfless, and with a sense of kindness, for these qualities allow him to render his service selflessly. This is the compensatory concept of emotional salary since sometimes it is certainly worth dying for something so that it is worth living.

> *"The purpose of life is to contribute in some*
> *way to making things better."*
> **Robert F. Kennedy**
> American politician and lawyer

Slackline, walking on the rope, is a fascinating sport of discipline since it brings an implicit message: the balance we need for our daily living. Among the benefits that the practice of this sport can generate are elasticity, flexibility, concentration, management of body forces, joint strength, and consciousness of the body. Metaphorically, the purposeful servant's training is the same: fall, learn to rise and continue to maintain balance, that much-needed emotional balance to start improving your moral ability so as not to fall into a vacuum.

The scattered servant

"Say what we feel, feel what we say,
match the words with the mind."

Seneca
Roman philosopher, statesman, and dramatist

The scattered servant is the malicious distracted one who consciously acts with indifference during a conversation or procedure with the user, who has to suffer almost daily with such servants.

This condition can be the product of emotional situations, scattered attention syndrome, hyperactivity, or organizational culture. It is worrying that the user encounters people who develop their activity isolated from reality, distracted, and, in many cases, with a deviated gaze towards their mobile phone or social networks. It is impossible to offer a good service if there is no concentration on the requests and needs of the other. Many times, when the user finishes telling his story, the servant asks him again or demands that he repeat the information, as he was not attentive to what was requested. Naturally, on many occasions, the citizen is unclear, but that is not common.

This attitude means that queries, questions, observations, and concerns are not compatible with the user's needs, who ends up in an abyss. A conversation with a dispersed servant generates uncertainty, tiredness, lack of motivation to solve problems, and disorientation.

Imagine receiving a service from health or justice professionals with a servant of this magnitude. A sparse servant can cause terrible damage to society, and the consequences are unpredictable. The absence of concern and interest in providing a good service harms the user significantly.

How to not be one?

This subtitle warns us that our work is part of a personal commitment. Let us then discover our efficiency, loyalty, willingness, and a good understanding of solidarity through sincere service. A purposeful servant, who acts with professional ethics, is kind and concerned, will have cosmic compensation. His performance will make him more prominent in ethical principles, his best allies.

The friendly servant

*"When given the choice between
being right or being kind, choose kind."*
R J Palacio
American author

A friendly treatment entails social advantages since it counteracts aggression, physical and symbolic violence, and abuse. In a society as hectic as the one we live in, in which time is not enough to exchange with others, the skills that

contribute to making relationships with others more rewarding are of great importance. Today, cordial and empathetic treatment has moved into the background, but kindness is an attribute of great importance to servants.

Putting kindness into practice is no easy task. We often hear the user's complaints about the lack of kindness, as the service is increasingly impersonal in this hectic world. Therefore, indecorous and often proud, arrogant, and rude behaviors take advantage; day by day, we suffer them, and the negative effect of this lack on our society is often appreciated.

A kind attitude is identified with affection, solidarity, and understanding. These are values that we must recover urgently to develop a better service interaction. Cordial acts are part of kindness and help forge it into one's own character. You can do simple exercises like shaking hands, smiling, thinking about each other, listening without making judgments, offering apologies, and thanking. At the end of the day, they will generate an incredible feeling of well-being and satisfaction in the servant for achieving a good job performance.

In short, kindness is a social skill that must be developed and implemented without expecting reciprocity. It is an expression of fair treatment and respect for others.

"Whatever you think
I think good words are not too much."
William Shakespeare
English playwright

Medical studies indicate that solidarity promotes physical and emotional health and improves the quality of life.

Do not have a hard time saying thank you! Scholars show that pronouncing these words without exaggeration provides happiness and strengthens relationships.

"Showing affability unites people in networks of reciprocal obligations, and it is an easy way to strengthen relationships that are often overlooked," says Robert Emmons, professor of psychology at the University of California Davis (USA).

In addition, when kindness is expressed, the feeling of community is improved, that is, the degree of commitment felt towards the other. Being kind is a way to be respectful of others.

In the work aspect, it is elementary to be kind. It increases the value of work, and it harmonizes the work environment and interpersonal relationships with colleagues.

Stephanie Brown, a psychologist at the University of Michigan, assures us that giving induces positive sensations and reduces stress.

The friendly servant builds confidence for a happy life, which is an essential requirement for a fluid daily interaction that improves the quality of our lives.

"We only really learn what we share with someone."
Leon Tolstoy
Russian writer

The dispute over the word

"I think the first virtue is to restrain the tongue;
he approaches nearest to gods who knows how to be silent,
even though he is in the right."

Cato
Roman statesman

It is inappropriate behavior not to let people talk and not know how to listen to the other. This behavior is part of the "culture of inculturation," as stated by the Chilean philosopher Emilio Galán. The circumstances of the culture of desire in which our society lives today overshadow the principle of listening to each other and providing space to express ourselves.

Often, the user suffers this misfortune because of an impatient servant, which impedes him from properly exposing his needs, which significantly affects the service.

"If you contribute to other people's happiness,
you will find the true goal,
the true meaning of life."
Dalai Lama
Buddhist spiritual leader

The dispute over the word usually occurs because of power. It is not a new phenomenon in the human condition and is part of the culture of selfishness.

Not letting the other speak is a manifestation of wanting to be right about everything, regardless of others' opinions. In this way, one person can seem aggressive because wanting to be right extends in the speech, without keeping pauses, and without taking into account the needs of the other, his interlocutor.

Knowing how to respect the turn to speak when the user has it is essential to provide a good service. The key is to "grow together and start thinking that we can all be one," as Miriam Subiriana, a Spanish coach, argues. Do not let circumstances dominate you, so it will be easier to know how to reach consensus and share the user and servant's purposes; in other words, reaching agreements.

Do not deny your emotions; better drive them wisely to grow as a person and become an assertive servant; this is to express your feelings calmly, identifying every emotion that arises. Thus you will have a smooth and balanced conversation according to the interests of both parties.

In many cases, whether in family, personal, business, or other relationship, when a person takes the word, it is possible to notice an act from the ego, which leads to disrespect and even abuse. Knowing how to interact at the right time inspires ease and transparency and clarifies the idea that users propose.

Do not abuse when you have the word and, when the other person has it, be respectful, know how to listen because the desire not to let speak does not allow you to concentrate and makes you a scattered servant.

The word is welcome when used without offense, without abuse, without injuries, without misrepresentation, and always to contribute, build, and create a bridge that serves as a consensus for greater understanding. Control your words; a servant who enjoys this virtue is the only author in his mind, decides and establishes proper management of his expressions, and controls his destiny.

As a servant, you, and no one else, are responsible for the word you say. Do not use it to stigmatize, nor abuse it when you have it in the face of the opportunity you have received from the other. Not letting talk does not give you more power; it does not elevate your status. It is a privilege to have spaces to manifest beliefs and a balanced opportunity to speak, with interlocution, and it will generate a good understanding between the parties. Because of their power, some media outlets believe themselves to own the word, and they cause a lot of damage. Pope Francis argues that "the media must be clear and transparent and without the intention to offend."

Be aware that providing a responsible service includes speaking at the right time and allowing the other to express himself. If you put yourself in the user's role, you will know how to handle this aspect because you will understand that you feel better when you have been listened to with attention, respect, and genuine receptiveness. Additionally, it is essential to listen to "the inner voice," use your intuition when listening to a user and try to help them honestly. Intuition lies in silence, and attentive listening will give you clear clues about the best way to solve difficulties. It is time; review your attitude and thinking to find out how to improve in this regard.

How to avoid war over the right to speak?

To solve this question, we need to talk about the ability to focus. As a servant, concentrate on paying attention and focus on a particular activity. It is a matter of decision; control your "words" and do not talk more than you should; use it in a timely and positive manner. Once you clarify in your consciousness how your interest works by listening to others, you can change your attitude and control your power of concentration to use it properly.

Be aware of your interior. It is a simple process that will help you be a more humane and responsive person for the user.

Perform emotional exercises and use all moral techniques to develop this goal laudably. Grow, change, it is a matter of interest.

"You have to manage emotions as if it were a social problem
and build social bonds."
Emiliana Simon-Thomas
Good Science Center

The listening servant enjoys empathetic reception and understands others, capturing in his essence what they feel and think. He is the servant who is willing to listen carefully to the partner or client when providing a good service.

The patient who goes to a doctor to check the symptoms of pain or illness he or she is suffering needs to find a health care professional willing to listen. Otherwise, this servant is absent from the sense of empathetic reception because knowing how to listen is a gift that benefits those who receive the service.

Imagine the doctor who is already formulating a prescription without letting the patient explain in detail and thoroughly the ailments he has been suffering. Often the health servant interrupts him without allowing him to finish his account and orders examinations without knowing the background of the disease.

To know how to listen, we must free ourselves from all prejudice about the person and his actions. Listening to others involves an exercise of silence, prudence, total concentration, interest in the appreciations received by the person who needs to be heard. Listening to others is not easy; the best way to do this is to essentially consider three aspects: zero reproaches, zero personal comments, and zero prejudices. Just listen.

When we listen, we must refrain from manifesting expressions that could injure the other person, such as 'I warned you,' 'I would have done something different instead,' 'that's not the way things were,' 'poor you,' 'pity that you were so stubborn,' etc. It is just about listening with all the senses, with your mind, just listening. Only when the other person is genuinely heard will there be a real space for dialogue.

The servant, whatever his business position, whose mission has to do with attention to the user, must implement the above assessments because empathetic reception allows him to know how to listen and understand those who receive the service of the competent administration. A servant that knows how to listen to his partner will know how to do it before the community.

How to conduct your tasks with discipline?

Efficiency and depth of thought will significantly help a servant commit to optimizing his work activity by prioritizing his goals with discipline. Thus, it is advisable to maintain an orderly agenda that will prevent anxiety and impatience, feelings that might limit his emotional skills when, in truth, his social purpose should lead him to the culmination of his duties successfully.

The best way for a servant to best conduct his tasks is with discipline, the ability to solve complex situations, and prioritizing his ideas. A good servant acts consistently and avoids being distracted by other things. We know that the human brain can store an infinity of information in a lifetime. Still, when expressing such information, the strict sense of ordering each thought is imposed. Time plays an extraordinary role here, the infinitesimal space of time that memory requires. Bifurcated the path of this thought, it is not uncommon for the person to say, "What were we talking about...?"

The internet, smartphones and tablets, the tendency to communicate on WhatsApp, and to keep an eye on social media have led scientists to investigate how this overloading of information affects the brain. And they have discovered that, from a biological point of view, there is little that can be done.

Even if our brain's capabilities are limitless, today's incredible living system puts it to the test. And here is a dilemma; the pragmatism that the whole world seems to depend on overruns the volume of our capacity and goodwill. Nervousness takes hold of us, and unlucky words emerge in our vocabulary. So our mission will be to make our words sweet because we might have to repent of them tomorrow.

"We have created a society with which our brain
can no longer deal efficiently."
Earl Miller
MIT scientist

The Art of Serving with Happiness consists of fine-tuning ideas and invite concentration. "One can cook and talk on the phone at the same time. The problem arises when trying to do three things at once," say other studies that confirmed the inability of the human being to be efficient in more than two tasks at once.

The cause of bad service is often associated with these sorts of behaviors, which induce the servant to make mistakes of all significance. In the face of the sudden change from one idea to another, creativity diminishes and thought deviates, convincing ourselves of what we do or say when in truth, we are not adequately concentrated.

"When people think they are multitasking, they are actually just switching from one task to another very rapidly. And every time they do, there is a cognitive cost in doing so," explains Earl Miller. I always see people driving hands-free, thinking that they solve the problem, but they do not. When one is focused on a conversation over the phone, one is not focused on the road, even though the brain gives the illusion that it is, scholars argue.

A concentrated servant does better, and his serviceability is appreciated when he tries to search for spaces in a quiet and noise-free environment, where attention does not deviate. Technological distractions in this information age damage IQ; working in a noisy environment is not the same as in a silent one, its best ally. When this conclusion is reached, every effort is made to provide a good service. It means that order in the tasks has been reached.

My best recommendation in this information age is not to enter the culture of addiction by working on various things at the time so as not to lose your concentration; it is a matter of awareness. It is of utmost importance for the servant to solve more complex tasks and properly prioritize his activities.

> *"What a restful life is that of the one who flees from the worldly noise, following the hidden path that the few sages who have been in the world have gone."*
> **Fray Luis de León**
> Spanish lyric poet, Augustinian friar,
> theologian, and academic

CHAPTER II

The servant and its condition

The authenticity of the servant

"Be original, authentic,
and be there for others."
Juan Carlos Ramirez
Mexican politician

As a servant, have you ever wondered how many times a day you put on a mask to show a face that is not yours but what you are interested in projecting?

There are no workers exempt from doing so; however, it is harmful to use a mask continuously. Welcome to authenticity! It gives confidence and security to those who embrace it. The worker's mask is an excuse to hide and not appearing as one is, not to provide the service as it should be, which often leads to malicious behavior, helpful in committing acts of corruption.

Being authentic will help you be a better worker.

"If there are no personality changes or even with major modifications to move forward, it is good to be genuine, meaning do not fake."
Jack and Suzy Welch
American business executives

Appearing to have qualities, attributes, or service skills using lies is a consequence of a servant's lack of authenticity. Be authentic, do not pretend, be yourself! Being authentic will favor you in your personal growth and providing a straight, honest, and transparent service. Sometimes servants become obsessed with doing or having. To achieve their end, they appear to possess values. Using their mask permanently, they deceive the user or the person requesting the service and show him what has not yet been finalized or present a false "truth." In many cases, these behaviors lead the recipient of the service to inappropriate decisions. "It is not about you being someone you are not; it is about potentializing those strengths that make you unique and transmitting them..." said Jeff Bezos, Founder of Amazon.

What is the servant expecting with these performances or social masks?

With these actions, the servant seeks to guarantee his benefit because acting this way does not benefit others. An authentic servant does not put up a front to provide good service, as he is aware that it violates the dignity, ethics, and trust the community placed in him.

The absence of authenticity does not clearly show what is behind the mask or the servant's real face. He makes his front his best ally and appears to be serving as it should; he pretends to look good even if the customer is the injured one by not receiving what he requires appropriately. An authentic servant accepts mistakes and apologizes, as he can acknowledge his mistakes when his conscience tells him to. The lack of authenticity implies questionable behavior, which becomes part of the work personality.

For the authentic servant, the idea of having a model or seeking advice from someone he respects is never harmful; this doesn't stop him from being himself. Originality is key, says business magnate, investor, and philanthropist Richard Branson. Even to laugh, one has to be authentic. Robin Dunbar, professor of evolutionary psychology at the University of Oxford, argues: "The laughter capable of relieving is the genuine, the laughter; not the courtesy giggles, let alone the cocktail laughs." Your best brand is you; your stamp makes you unique as a servant, so you will achieve success in what you undertake and help others improve.

> *"The identity of a person consists simply in being and being cannot be denied."*
> ***José Saramago***
> Portuguese writer

The servant who believes to own the truth

"Three things are destructive in life: anger, greed, and excessive self-esteem."

Muhammad
Religious leader, founder of Islam

The servant that assumes to have the last word harms the whole company. Holding meetings, committees, boards of directors, among other group activities, is impossible when there are people with these disrespectful and almost pathological behaviors. Listening is not their preferred activity and, despite being aware of their mistake, pride does not allow them to stop and reflect on the importance of such action.

The truth is not the exclusive property of the servant. Therefore, a person with these characteristics must realize that this attitude does a lot of damage to any business project.

The servant who believes himself to own the truth makes whimsical decisions, which does not allow him to analyze and interpret situations correctly, leading to unfair assessments.

Logical and self-critical reasoning of himself would help him draw favorable conclusions for his projects. The servant who does not believe in possessing the truth is aware that his critical and equitable thinking impacts exemplary service to the community. On the contrary, a servant "owner" of the truth departs from good service through improvisations, decisions lacking objectivity, stubbornness, and continuous whims.

A change in attitude would favor this type of servant both personally and workwise because arrogance would no longer take advantage; on the contrary, it would become humility, which would help in spiritual and emotional growth, an essential attitude to avoid that kind of behavior.

Whoever believes himself the owner of the truth does not purge information, does not investigate, does not analyze, is carried away by prejudice or misguided opinions, and does not give importance to the evidence. He feels that his word is infallible; he does not accept reproaches from his work environment because his ego is so big that the only truth he admits is his own.

Thales of Miletus, a Greek mathematician, astronomer, and philosopher, claimed that greed and arrogance are the principal vices of the powerful. Requesting help or guidance, or hearing a recommendation, does not diminish the person's authority or capacity. On the contrary, it denotes humility, and it does not mean to be less or downgraded to others, says the Spaniard Emilio Gómez López, creator and director of "Stratos."

A servant free from all prejudice listens and does not think his word is absolute. Listening to others implies an exercise of silence, of interest in feedback, provided that what is heard is based on serious criteria, authentic, transparent, objective, and close to the truth.

Some servants like to receive constant flattery as it sweetens their ears and makes them believe that they are always right even if they are wrong. At that moment, their inner self, their self-criticism, must act and point out an awareness through which to exercise the spirit of providing a better service.

When pride takes hold, one must emotionally evolve from the learning of outstanding people to turn snubs into consensus. Weaknesses must also be positively shifted into strengths. A servant who does not believe to be the owner of the truth proposes goals, accepts feedback, and reaches agreements. Taking into account all of the above is an invaluable investment in the quality of work.

> *"Hire people who are really good*
> *at things you're not good at."*
> **Susan Lyne Hog Ventures**
> Founder and President of BBG Ventures

Values are principles that govern human behavior; they are the pillars of society and the way its customers act. Also, by being consistent with them, the best contribution will be made.

The servant and the abuse of his role

"We are what we repeatedly do.
Excellence, then, is not an act, but a habit."

Aristotle
Greek philosopher

While the servant is unclear about his sense of equality, it will be impossible for him to be unbiased in his actions, and he will abuse the position he holds. Believing to be superior is the product of a society where discrimination pollutes the environment almost daily. The issue of inclusion is not given the value it deserves, which allows some servants, both private and public, to border on this kind of abuse of the human condition.

In this context, discrimination can be seen as a reflection of family attitudes that transcend all social spheres. These attitudes are given with greater emphasis today, as we live in an empire of taste for easy money, favoring the absence of values—especially when they are as endangered as freshwater dolphins—and allows corruption to tarnish the clear crystal of morality, governor of ethical behaviors.

"The real danger of being on top
is the fall."
Albert Figueroa
Autonomous University
Barcelona Spain

The servant that ignores inclusion abuses his position at all levels. Again, believing yourself superior, expressed not only in words but with gestures, derogatory body language, or sometimes with physical outrage, is an attribute of the servant's arrogance, as harmful to those who receive the service as to the institution. Those who are clear about their sense of service know the principle of equality because they assume a comprehensive mission conduct, which has a significant impact on their social interaction as much as in the workplace. Thus, simplicity, without losing the missionary beacon, is part of their realization. Without humility, it is impossible for a servant not to abuse his condition. The essence of the service is respect, transparency, and kindness with an active disposition. In this order of ideas, inclusion should be a habit, a value that favors providing a better service.

A servant motivated in his condition aims at transparency for his company's growth. When he abuses his condition, it becomes routine to influence other people in an almost obsessive way, to change their thinking and acting. He continually seeks to be respected, to make his authority prevail, and to impose his ideas at all costs. These types of servants speak at all times in terms of 'I decide,' 'I impose,' and 'the last word is mine.' They have little interest in listening to others. Their excessive motivation for power leads them to abuses of authority and the imposition of inappropriate ideas and procedures. Probably many of the servant's corruption problems are driven by an act of immense need to attain power and not by the need to achieve his goals.

The servant who does not abuse his condition desires to serve efficiently, based on the fulfillment of the objectives and the proposed goals. The position of this type of servant is outside the abuse of power, and he aspires to find solutions to problems and manage them well. In contrast, arrogant servants damage the integrity of the service.

Using an identification to cover up any misconduct also constitutes an abuse of authority by the servant. In these cases, it is both the servant's and the recipient's responsibility. As a user, you must be very careful not to fall into dishonest acts. The servant should not have preferences, as these are the product of an exclusive society.

It should be noted that thanking arouses a degree of responsibility in the other. Researchers argue that one should thank 'without exaggerating,' as sometimes this becomes sickening. For example, when thanking someone is compensated for no reason, it can be interpreted as a need to "buy" them because their approval is needed, either out of insecurity or for consideration if they ever need that person. We must be grateful when the favor done is selfless, and that gratitude must be consonant with the service provided. It is unnecessary to thank when the work has implied compensation, payment, or agreement, although a cordial "thank you" is never too much.

Those who receive the service must not have a hard time saying thank you. According to clinical physical psychologist José Elías, giving thanks is a way to be respectful of others. It is also a way to strengthen affective bonds.

The important thing for a servant who does not abuse his role is to be clear that he is there to serve and that his service is always to benefit those who require it.

> *"He who has truth at his heart need never fear the want of persuasion on his tongue."*
> **John Ruskin**
> English philosopher, social thinker,
> and philanthropist

CHAPTER III

The servant and his attitudes

Sensitivity and wisdom in the art of serving

"Of all the means that lead to fortune, the safest is perseverance and work."

Marie R. Reybaud

French writer, politician, and political economis

People chart their path to success or failure by the disposition of their mood, which is called attitude. The right attitude to success is a mental disposition with a positive meaning. The contrary or inappropriate, which usually leads to failure, is a negative mental attitude. Within this context, servants can move toward success or failure when adopting appropriate or inadequate attitudes, respectively.

*"He who knows others is wise.
He who knows himself is enlightened."*

Lao-Tzu

Chinese philosopher

The servant facing human rights

"We are our worst enemy. Nothing can destroy humanity except humanity itself."

PierreTeilhard de Chardin

French priest

Human rights are based on the dignity of the person. They are understood as the fundamental faculties, prerogatives, and freedoms that the person has simply because of being so, without which one cannot live as such. They are characterized by being inalienable and imprescriptible. Therefore, every human being, regardless of race, color, sex, language, religion, political opinion, national or social origin, economic position, birth, or any other condition, must enjoy them and can claim their recognition, respect, guardianship, and promotion on the part of all.

"The secret of peace is respect
for human rights."
John Paul II
Pope of the Catholic Church
from 1978 until 2005

"If it is a duty to respect the rights of others,
it is also a duty to uphold one's own."
Herbert Spencer
English philosopher

The struggle for these rights is inherent in the provision of service, respecting and providing a dignified, adequate treatment without exclusion, taking into account that preferences in service are a faithful reflection of the ignorance of the dignity of the person. The servant must be clear in that giving value to the concept of the humane, and recognizing that set of rights that the person has, is one of the main challenges facing his mission.

"Virtue is a kind of health, beauty,
and good habit of the soul."
Plato
Greek philosopher

The servant must have the disposition to talk, to find solutions to disagreements, and a process of continuous improvement. When the customer recognizes human rights in a servant's work, the servant is even more motivated to perform his tasks. We cannot ignore that there is a person behind each user, and through his mission, the servant is the first to respect the rights of the client to give real value to the concept of the human being.

*"Every human act explicitly or implicitly contains
a relationship with moral norms."*
José Luis Vásquez Borau
Spanish author

For being a subject of interest and great significance, it is recommended to use the critical thinking mentioned in the corresponding section of this book. With the knowledge you possess and depending on it, you may or may not agree with the above; however, the real interest is that everyone grasps the essence of what was raised, concludes, reflects, and implements what they can to give the best in this regard.

Every servant needs to improve their personal life and a good performance in human and social aspects. If you cultivate human relations, trust, respect, equality, justice, solidarity, and good communication, you invest in building respect for fundamental rights. A more humane servant dignifies his nature and meaning as a person.

*"To live honorably, to harm no one,
and to give to each his own."*
Ulpian
Roman jurist

The servant that enjoys the pain of others:
How to change this attitude?

*"There is nothing that mediocre people hate more
than the superiority of talent."*
Stendhal
French writer

This type of servant disguises himself with a hypocritical smile and enjoys what might happen to his co-workers. The servants that enjoy the pain of others are intolerable, constantly with a sour face, always aware of any slip to come up with a scathing comment or an unfair critique.

They are the ones who mock you and even make excessive comments in front of the boss and enjoy the warnings that may result. The truth is that many servants of this kind surround us.

The servants with these features are critics who wait for you to make a mistake to say "inept!" on your face or for you to say something out of tune to make faces before others.

They are those who have the phrase "I told you so," ready as if it were their wild card to ridicule you. These servants have a language that is part of their "work self" and includes words such as "dumbass," "slow," "useless," and "stupid," among others. They enjoy warnings or terminations of contracts or the investigations their peers may be subjected to due to the promoted slander or insult. These servants commit countless acts, and the symbol that identifies them is an air of triumph when others do poorly because, that way, they do not feel that they are the bad ones.

> *"Kindness is loving people more than they deserve."*
> **Joubert**
> French moralist and essayist

The attitude of the offended servant

This attitude must entail some indifference, for silence and prudence are best in the face of grievances and evil. It is necessary to manage emotions before getting aggressive; the higher the offense, the higher the mindfulness.

The servant and self-esteem

> *"Never injure a friend, even in jest."*
> **Marcus Tullius Cicero**
> Roman statesman and lawyer

A servant who is unhappy with his work, who believes he has little skills or little capacity for job growth, develops a sense of guilt, enters routine, has little interest in becoming better, and loses self-respect. To improve self-esteem in the workplace, the attitude must be modified by projecting a desire for improvement, zero negative thoughts, undertaking actions of change, and developing activities that allow you to interact with affection and respect.

A servant with high self-esteem is characterized by valuable ideas for the benefit of himself, which directly and indirectly impact the company in which he works; he has clear objectives to move forward and is motivated to achieve what is proposed within the company. He competes with himself in the face of his potentiality to prove himself; he has momentum and enjoys a positive force that generates confidence and enthusiasm that contributes to realizing what he wants concerning his personal, social, and work success.

A servant without self-esteem acclaims the virtues and forgives the mistakes and defects of others. Still, he is unfair, cruel, and demanding with himself, which leads to unsatisfactory job performance, a feeling that prevents him from improving.

Those servants who feel under-performed with their activities must recognize the qualities that allow them to feel good and put them into practice within their company. Nominators should adjust selection processes to place employees according to their competencies.

If, despite everything, you are in the situation described above, change your attitude; turn in your favor all the energy you invest in saying to yourself that you are not capable!

" He has a right to criticize,
who has a heart to help."
Abraham Lincoln
American statesman and lawyer
16th President of the United States

The servant with class

"There is no excess in the world so commendable
as excessive gratitude."
Jean de la Bruyere
French philosopher and moralist

The classy servant is the one who develops his work activity with inner dignity, which allows him to be complete, coherent, and objective in all his performances, and has a particular sensitivity to capture what his co-workers want, seek, or need. To have class is to be faithful, authentic to yourself and with your principles, and be more committed to the work environment.

Austrian neurologist and psychiatrist Viktor Frankl says: "Dignity and grace of the self is a test of maturity and freedom, indispensable when learning to lead. Governing yourself is essential to directing well."

Class cannot be just appearance; it is not purchased or boasted. Class comes from within; it is a kind of inner dignity; it involves empathy, simplicity, and energy. Anthony de Mello, an Indian Jesuit priest and psychotherapist, said: "Wisdom can be learned, but it cannot be taught."

"The most important quality of greatness is making a reality
of what we seem to be."
Socrates
Greek philosopher

The servant that never loses

This servant feels the need to seem invulnerable and perfect in the eyes of others. This is so because he believes that if he makes a mistake, he will lose the respect and affection of others and, if this happens, it would be impossible for him to live worthily. This kind of servant significantly harms the work environment, as he hurts the honesty and respect of someone when it comes to losing.

The fear of losing prompts him to give up a genuine encounter with the other. Despite never accepting that he has made a mistake, he always apologizes and, above all, injures his peers to defend his dignity by insulting or slandering them comfortably and calmly, without taking responsibility.

That is the case, for example, of the director or manager of a company requesting an employee's resignation. According to him, it is an order from higher management. He uses expressions such as "if you do not resign immediately, you will be removed through the termination of the contract." The employees facing a threat are forced to make such a determination, and one of them informs the presidency of the company, unaware of the situation. Subsequently, the manager who had requested the resignation expresses with great peace of mind that the workers did so of their own volition as if he had not been responsible for it. He is indifferent to the consequences that his actions may bring for the sole point of never losing when triumph is in his way.

Before these kinds of characters, the big losers are the employees or workers who harmoniously work because the "servants that never lose" go above any value, do not know the price of humility, and do not take a step back under any circumstances.

The servant with this characteristic is the one that constantly seeks to succeed, no matter the means to use. He acts according to himself, and the same thing happens in his interpersonal relationships. Making deals with his co-workers becomes difficult for him; therefore, someone's respect and honesty are almost always injured, as his inconvenient way of acting is unexpected by the affected. His behavior is disguised in the face of a desire to look perfect in front of others. He always wins, whatever it takes.

He hardly shows his mistakes or weaknesses. A servant set in not losing pretends to show logically and forcefully that those around him must change because, according to him, they are wrong; he never looks imperfect; he is always right and changes the rules of the game if he has a chance to lose. This servant finds it hard to recognize the evil he can cause others in the face of his responsibilities. When realizing that, intentionally or unintentionally, he has made mistakes, he prefers to resign rather than accept his responsibility.

There is no hesitation in maneuvering or manipulating situations when this servant is in leadership positions until he gets away with it. In many cases, a committee or board under his direction becomes a source of sour discussion when his proposals, even if they are wrong, are not accepted. He prefers to end the meeting, deferring it for the future to build his project to gain advantage and credibility with others, aware of his mistake.

Be flexible but firm; change for your sake and that of your organization. Overcoming the above requires a will for change for your own good and the entity served.

"Forgiveness is a process, not a moment."
Dr. Edward M. Hallowell
Harvard psychiatrist
author of "Dare to Forgive"

The angry servant

"He who dominates his anger dominates his worst enemy."
Confucius

Identifying anger allows us to know how to act to change the situation, promoting working relationships, and avoiding unpleasant or unfavorable consequences, both for the servant and the institution.

When we are angry, it is not easy to express the reason for it instantly. That is why today's servant is advised to handle this situation to avoid problems.

Psychiatrist Daniel Gutierrez argues: "The secret is to learn to control impulses and not explode immediately. Of course, it's not about holding and suppressing emotions; it's about knowing how to channel them properly."

It is necessary, first of all, to pause. We then face two options: remain silent, refraining from blaming or encouraging the punishment of other colleagues, that is, to act prudently, or react aggressively or violently, shouting or mistreating the partner or customer receiving the service. In the latter case, the ones that ultimately end up being harmed are both the institution and the servant who did not manage the situation. When you feel injured by a partner, a user, or your boss, go to the actions that will allow you to defend yourself. That will prevent the causes that can generate sanctions and go as far as disengagement from office.

The wrath of others is not the only disturbing thing. Learn how to control yours by following the steps recommended by anger management expert Ron Potter-Efron. Next time you feel you are about to lose control, try this: "To avoid saying anything you might regret, take time to calm down. Avoid face-to-face conflict, especially in front of colleagues. If someone verbally offends you during an argument, put some distance between you instead of becoming defensive. Tell him you'd rather discuss it later."

Write down a list of attitudes for anger management. Write down six things to do when you feel angry; for example, breathing, slowing down, trying to listen to the other person, not screaming, and holding bad words. Read it whenever you need it.

If you knew, as a servant, how much you gain by considering these recommendations, you would avoid ongoing problems and benefit, not only your work life but your personal life as well, which is the most important thing. Before being a good servant, you have to know how to be a person. Do not forget that anger is contagious, and if a conflict arises, everyone is affected, and people may tend to take sides. The wisest thing to do is to take angry employees out of sight and the ears of their co-workers. Thus, it is possible to remain under control and impartial when handling a situation before collaborators or when a partner is affected by anger. You should also act similarly to avoid getting involved in the rage of others.

"Anger has a destructive and evil character," says the Dalai Lama. An example of work anger is that of a boss who imposes his will by force. Servant friend, the most important thing is to ask yourself what anger is good for and how it benefits you at work. The conclusion must be obvious: not good at all!

> *"Hate produces fear,*
> *from fear you move to offense."*
> **Niccolò Machiavelli**
> Renaissance Italian diplomat

The servant that enjoys his work activity

*"Life passes, fast caravan! Stop then your mount
and try to be happy."*
Omar Khayyam
Persian mathematician, astronomer,
philosopher, and poet

This servant identifies with a culture of values and commitment to the institution or company. He is always motivated by positivism, allowing him to be cooperative, participatory, loyal, enthusiastic, responsible, creative, honest, stable, confident, optimistic, and mature. That is how he enjoys work and develops his activity better than expected.

The servant at the management level must handle his self-control very well, setting an example with his excellent behavior and avoiding falling into errors that make him a hinderer or ignorant of the institutional mission.

Daniel Goleman, an American psychologist, author, and science journalist, presents the following recommendations to enjoy the working activity:

- Be aware of your emotions, understanding the feelings of others.
- Tolerate the pressures and frustrations you can withstand.
- Adopt an empathetic and social attitude to find personal development.

Change in attitude

It is necessary to change your attitude, that is, to visualize horizons that allow you to set new goals, having a positive vision of the future, and knowing that man will always be a being in search of perfection. The best change is becoming a planner for better results based on diagnosing situations and defining goals. Teamwork is also essential as a group of two or more people who regularly interact to fulfill a common purpose and, above all, seek to develop the same action systematically, unifying criteria, using the same methodology to meet their goals and thus achieving them with established strategies. Some hypotheses regarding the change of organizations are based on people's desire to grow and develop their potential for work to the fullest. So the success of the organization where you work is up to you. Planning is critical for change, according to the schedule you have within your goals.

> " *Wisdom is knowing what to do next.*
> *Virtue is doing it.*"
> **David Starr Jordan**
> Founding president of Stanford University

An unplanned change can become a destructive element for the organization, hence the importance of taking into account that any transformation must imply a difference in the attitude of the servants. A universal goal for change is to get servants to learn how to diagnose their actions to analyze situations and plan for change. Without planning, change is disastrous for the company.

> *"Trust is worth gold."*
> **Francis Fukuyama**
> American political scientist

The tardy servant

"Punctuality is the politeness of kings."
Louis XVIII
King of France

Lack of punctuality is an ordinary evil among top managers of companies or institutions, who, according to USA Today, are late for eight out of ten meetings. Tardiness at work is more than a sign of rudeness. The time wasted due to delays because of servant absences is one of the leading causes of lost revenue.

Being late makes a bad impression on employers or bosses and shows a lack of consideration for others. Similarly, always being late can tarnish your reputation with friends and colleagues, despite being a respected servant; in such a case, it is easy for them to overlook your good qualities. Tardiness can affect the servant's other virtues.

In addition to being disrespectful, tardiness distracts others. Perhaps, too, it may give the impression that one considers oneself superior. As a result, some executives tend to be late for meetings and believe they give importance to their position by being untimely. They believe their lateness gives their positions more status. Regardless of the administrative and disciplinary consequences, their image deteriorates before the institution and society.

Recommendation: Learn how to manage your time well, make a list of your pending activities, set priorities, calculate how long they will take, and when you can, carry them out.

The servant arriving early at the job site sets an example before his collaborators allowing them to be obliged to adequately perform their functions without the need for pressures or rules imposing a schedule within the institution.

Getting to all commitments on time should become a habit for the servant.

Where is the respect for other people's time?

The Honest Servant

"The object of the superior manis truth."
Confucius
Chinese philosopher

A servant with a moral sense does not disguise himself. If you know yourself, listen openly and confess to your intuitions frankly, you will be able to give everything of yourself. For your company, the institutional commitment is with yourself.

Being honest is not a mind game to put a good face on things. To be politically correct is to pay attention to what your heart tells you to be true, says Robert Cooper, a British diplomat and adviser. The honest servant is contrary to the double moral servant, who always has a mask on and never presents himself as he is.

Many are the damages that these workers create for society. Their actions are contrary to their inner truth. Aware of the harm they cause, they never accept it. A servant who is not honest about his behavior as a person, much less will do better as a servant, pretending to develop his work activity with decorum, appearing before society as a trustworthy servant. He does not accept his mistakes, blames others for them, and ignores the best values a servant with moral sense must have: sincerity, truth, and inner honesty.

An honest servant is honest with his conscience to make things right. Reflections on the poor performance of his functions or mistakes allow him to be a servant with a moral sense: he develops his working potential with integrity. When you listen wisely to your truth, you bring the best value that a good servant must have: honesty. Being honest is to preserve the trust that society gives you by standing out with irreproachable deeds and being above all doubt.

*"If you live your life the right way, the results will take
care of themselvesand dreams will come to you."*
Randy Pausch
American educator

Integrity is measured by what is fair and right, according to the principles that guide them. Like standards and ethics, among other tenets, integrity must also be based on independence, making decisions in line with social interest, and applying honest criteria. Being honest is a commitment to yourself, the institution, and society. An honest servant must be an example of righteousness.

*"Wealth is not his that has it,
but his that enjoys it."*
Benjamin Franklin
Founding father of the United States

The organized servant

*"Succes is a journey, not a destination.
The doing is often more important than the outcome."*
Arthur Ashe
American tennis player

This type of servant tenaciously develops his purposes, knows how to divide his work into tasks that make sense, schedules and creates checkpoints to measure his progress, and establishes clear lines of planning, order, and discipline.

The organized servant delegates tasks to himself, emphasizing the characteristics of the desired results and not merely their compliance. The most important thing for him is identifying the steps in his organization process, which transcends the work. He also practices continuously and takes on tasks related to his work. "If I do what I plan, I have the authority to delegate to others," some people argue.

In the case of the boss with this skill, he must ensure that his team is organized to develop their tasks, thus contributing to the company's purposes. An organized boss makes it easier for his collaborators or group to meet goals, determines how many people are needed to perform an activity, knows how to assign tasks, and when delegating a project, he makes sure his collaborators understand what he expects.

The critically thinking servant

> *"Autocontrol and learning to obey are tests of maturity*
> *necessary to know how to lead."*
> **Juan Manuel Parra Torres**
> INALDE Bussiness School

The critically thinking servant does not act impulsively or makes decisions based on whims, rumors, or prejudices. A critically thinking servant favors the customer by knowing how to receive, analyze, and interpret information before acting, question what he reads and hears, evaluate the quality of the information and use logical reasoning to draw conclusions.

The critically thinking servant can naturally interpret, analyze, and deduce all the data that comes to his job to provide excellent and fast solutions effectively and efficiently. By assessing a situation or problem, he can draw a conclusion and explain how he has reached it; he is aware that his sense of critical thinking impacts the provision of an objective, impartial and equitable service.

This type of servant makes sure to collect all the evidence and takes the time to think about and analyze it. Improvisations, reckless decisions, easiness are not of his preference. He is conscious that a hasty determination affects good service, so he is always willing to have an open mind that allows him to find information that will change his perspective of the problem.

The critical thinking servant's honesty allows him to recognize trends and prevent them from influencing him, being careful not to give more value to opinions than evidence. He can prevent the trafficking of influences or interests, which harm society, by realizing when someone favors a proposal but could hide personal reasons.

This servant is organized, debugs the information he collects, sets a criterion for evaluating it, writes the crucial points or things he might investigate later, considers and analyzes all possibilities. This feature is the most important of critical thinking; only after examining the options can you decide which is the best.

The servant with these qualities sees difficulties as a challenge and finds immediate solutions. His practice in critical thinking skills gives him security, confidence, and a sense of service. In this kind of servant, patience involves logic, reason, and reflection and using these tools to make the best decisions in every aspect. No doubt, being organized in the way of thinking gives transparency to his work as a servant.

The dissociating servant

"To know how many are jealous of you, count your admirers."
Seneca
Roman philosopher

The dissociating servant is the one that hinders business development but takes care of gaining indulgences with his superiors through flattery and by undoing his co-workers. These workers are notorious in all companies; they seek to emerge through questionable strategies without measuring the consequences. Their world is intrigue and resentment; they celebrate inappropriate actions and even bad jokes to win gifts, whether with their bosses or colleagues; their activity is always carried out around gossip. There is no principle of institutional commitment for these servants; a servant without this value cannot give anything of himself to his company. In the absence of passion for his work, he becomes non-fulfilling of the objectives that every company demands. He carries out his activity according to discord.

On the contrary, the prudent servant is the one who performs his functions thoroughly while being aware of his duties and obligations. He laudably develops the goals set without affecting the working environment.

"Envy and hatred attack the soul; resentment completely covers it."
Alfonso López Caballero
Spanish writer

The arrogant servant:
How to change this attitude?

"From insolence, arrogance is born; from arrogance hate."
Marcu Tullius Cicero
Roman statesman and philosopher

Arrogance is a feature that affects the provision of service and damages work environments. It can be avoided with humility, an essential attitude, honesty, transparency, commitment, kindness, and respect for others. A humble and simple servant can be proud of his behavior. Being shielded against arrogance is the best tribute to humility.

"Humility allows us to be able to accept that we ignore something or that our knowledge is insufficient and therefore we are willing to listen to those who know more or have more experience," says the Spaniard Emiliano Gómez López, creator and director of the personal, professional, and business development company Stratos. Requesting help or guidance or hearing a recommendation does not diminish the person's authority or ability; on the contrary, it denotes humility on the servant, without being less than anyone or downgrading to others. Rafael Ortega Ryberg argues that: "Arrogance, instead of ensuring success, limits and isolates those who apply it and dismisses the talent of those who suffer from it." The arrogant servant is generally regarded as someone distant, who prefers his own ideas to those of others. Specialists claim that "being arrogant means belittling people and the contributions they make, and produces in them a feeling of inferiority, rejection, and anger," "...with this attitude undermines morale until the team is destroyed."

Some servants think they have a unique and correct answer to everything, ignore other people's opinions, and take a distant attitude toward the customer. Even if it is not his intention, what a servant of this class often achieves is being left alone and isolated. That does not mean that a person cannot defend his views; on the contrary, you can do so, as long as you do not believe always to be correct, know how to express yourself, and accept the criticism brought by the opportunity to learn and do things better.

Angel Lafuente, an expert in verbal techniques, states that: "Accepting criticism naturally and recognizing that we are fallible beings does not undermine our security or confidence; is a symptom of strength." The great danger of servant arrogance is that it can become a blocking or throttling factor in the advancement of projects. Similarly, it affects work harmony.

On the other hand, the humble servant has an objective view of the actual dimension of his skills and strengths, does not feel close to perfection, and does not create resentments in others. He is accessible, listens and values opinions, shares the triumph, and does not show the authority that comes from his position. He prefers, first and foremost, to lead from empathy, one of the qualities of an effective leader and which means in this globalized world, to "understand the different cultures to show respect for their values," as Jack Welch, an American business executive, points out. That allows you to know yourself well, understand your strengths and limitations, and have good relationships with others.

One of the great difficulties in changing arrogance is the absence of feedback. The arrogant servant is overvalued.

Avoiding this behavior requires a change in attitude. "Listening to the customer means that we can calmly repeat the opinion that we are presented even if we disagree. Until we repeatedly show óthers that we are interested in and invite the client to speak and listen to him with genuine interest, especially those who have been offended in the past, arrogant behavior cannot be modified," experts say.

Scholars warn that "humility is how a person's greatness, strength, and self-confidence manifest itself." Arrogance impairs harmony because it prevents the search for clear orientations for the best organizational development.

The servant who acknowledges his mistakes and often his ignorance, not trying to hide his mistakes with meaningless or empty rhetoric, lives up to the organization's progress. The arrogance of the servant leads him to take arbitrary measures being irresponsible with his activity.

Intelligence and technical skills are critical in job development, but when simplicity is involved, it enriches the servant's attitude. Scholars argue that "the deeper our wisdom, the greater our humility because we will be more aware of what little we know, compared to how much remains to be known. Moreover, for people of conscience, there is no greater encouragement to learn than to acknowledge one's ignorance humbly."

> *"A selfish man strives to talk about himself*
> *when you are dying to tell him about you."*
> **Jean Cocteau**
> French poet

The servant who listens and respects ideas other than his own is tolerant, conscious of not knowing everything and that his thinking is not the most valuable, nor his opinion the best. He learns from others and recognizes that arrogance does not favor the growth of the entity where he works. How many valuable proposals, initiatives, and contributions are often lost to the arrogance of some servants? "Another facet of humility is to behave as one more among equals; not to be more or less within the group to which we belong," researchers propose on these issues of human behavior. Humility is to admit that there will always be other people from whom we can learn something else.

> *"Temper is what gets most of us into trouble.*
> *Pride is what keeps us there."*
> **Mark Twain**
> American writer

The servant with a desire to improve

> *"God doesn't require us to succeed,*
> *he only requires that you try."*
> **Mother Teresa of Calcutta**
> Catholic nun and missionary

The servant with a sense of improvement is the one with precise, accurate projections and always towards a defined goal. His aspirations are his best friends, always with an attitude of change to improve every day for his benefit. His challenges keep him on alert to overcome mental laziness and not turn his work into a routine. Without being addicted to it, his work is carried out with mystique because he loves what he does.

His motto must be 'continuous research,' to place himself in a status that allows him to develop the proposed objectives. Competition must be with his capabilities, proving that overcoming himself is easy, with persistence and discipline in the face of what he wants.

Eduardo Angel Reyes, a management consultant, argues: "At certain times you have to make decisions, many of them difficult and high risk. The important thing is to weigh them objectively."

The servant with a sense of overcoming is the one with the ability to handle difficulties. Creativity, perseverance, effort, laboriousness are positive characteristics of these servants. The American Psychological Association recommends ten actions to deal with difficult situations:

1. Establish Relationships.
2. Avoid seeing the crisis as insurmountable obstacles.
3. Accept that change is part of life.
4. Move towards your goals.
5. Take decisive action.
6. Look for opportunities to discover yourself.
7. Cultivate a positive view of yourself.
8. Keep things in perspective.
9. Don't give up hope.
10. Take care of yourself.

Optimism, art, sense of humor, and intellectual development, among others, are factors that favor or potentialize the servant at difficult times.

> *"Whatever your mind can conceive and believe,*
> *it can achieve."*
> **Napoleon Hill**
> American self-help author

Servants with some work stability must not abuse circumstances by resting on their laurels, not growing emotionally, being indifferent to business policies, and considering themselves, with an almost acquired right, free to do and undo against principles, affecting the interests of institutions. Otherwise, the servant with a sense of improvement, although enjoying these prerogatives, does not abuse his position and becomes an exemplary servant.

Servants must be company caretakers and must love it as much as to regard it as their own. Their cause is the organization.

A servant with a sense of improvement develops his pro-work activity, no matter what position he holds. Scholars state that this servant profile is the one that: "proposes projects and puts them into practice, is results-oriented, faces uncertainty, challenges the conventional, is flexible, anticipates difficulties and, in general, takes the initiative; reflects in creative ideas and concrete actions to generate changes in both professional and business growth." A servant with a sense of overcoming differs from others or makes a difference because he goes beyond the ordinary; he is of a broader vision; being recursive and creative allows him to overcome any difficulty more quickly. The servant with a sense of overcoming seeks success through change, dealing with problems with a sense of analysis before deciding.

> *"Nothing makes one old so quickly as the ever-present thought*
> *that one is growing older."*
> **Georg Christoph Lichtenberg**
> German physicist and satirist

According to María Pallares, an expert in personal training, "people who are not satisfied with their work, have the responsibility to generate new actions to change the situation and achieve the expected results." The servant with a sense of improvement creates his own spaces to develop new projects without fear, without feeling self-conscious to freely express what he wants, without prejudices of any nature.

Professor Thomas Bateman, a specialist in organizational behavior and strategic leadership, and J. Michael Crant, Professor of Management and Organization at University of Notre Dame, define people with initiative by the following characteristics: they continually seek new opportunities; they have goals oriented to change, anticipate problems, act differently, take action, and venture despite uncertainty. They also persevere and persist in their efforts until they achieve tangible results.

Globalization and technological advances force the servant to be in constant development to respond effectively to reality.

Sensitivity is part of his environment, not authoritarian behavior, which injures integral service.

A servant with initiative has a sense of overcoming. The servant that develops his skills in the work context contributes to business progress.

The servant with a sense of improvement appropriates his and his companions' difficulties, acting with serenity, assuming the setbacks with a positive spirit. He wins if his attitude is calm, and he handles situations appropriately. Persistence in his projects with self-confidence, knowing how to direct his behavior with balance will provide him with better results.

"He who lost his faith has nothing more to lose."
Spanish proverb

The Evasive Servant

"Always tell the truth. That way, you don't have to remember what you said."
Mark Twain
American writer

Every day the user suffers the culture of 'it's not possible,' without any justification, by the person who provides the service. It is usual for the servant to tell the user, 'come in the afternoon,' 'come tomorrow,' 'that's not my job, ' 'come within a month,' 'my partner is on leave, or holiday,' 'opening hours are until six p.m.,' 'we have five minutes before closing time.' Imagine yourself in the latter case, on the weekend, with an urgent need to solve a situation of significant scope that becomes a calamity due to not receiving the appropriate service. In short, there are many inconveniences or difficulties a person has to face because of the evasiveness continually presented in the service.

The lack of sensitivity from certain servants is of concern in the case of healthcare. That, in addition to excessive bureaucracy, the unnecessary complications that make life impossible for customers or users, the extensive documentation required of them, and the long lines, without thinking about the time they are wasting, is what ultimately leads to corruption.

How to not be?

Put yourself in the shoes of a person who needs the service. How would you feel if this happened to you? Carry out your activity with real meaning, give everything of yourself, not acting evasively, with the simple argument of 'it is not my duty.' An integral servant must be willing to take responsibility for efficiency, give solutions, look for creative mechanisms or alternatives, and not avoid service. When the established goals of organizational culture and personal development are met, a tribute to value is paid. Without evasiveness, service is better.

The non-evasive servant assumes a position with a will to serve. Rachel Carson says, "whatever the end you pursue and whatever your abilities, without a strong motivation to put them into practice, that is, without emotional commitment, you don't get very far." A non-evasive servant listens carefully to the user's interests, giving timely and practical solutions to the request.

Servants have to demonstrate their commitment to sincere personal conviction. A servant that is passionately committed to his cause inspires total trust in society.

A non-evasive servant is concerned about his inner growth and has a vision of a just service committed to the non-abuse of others' personal interests or those of society.

The Creative Servant

"To succeed, you have to learn to think."
Ivar Giaever
Norwegian-American physicist

We cannot be overcome by mental laziness, whose ally is routine. Working daily with this attitude will not allow you to develop different projects for the company. Your ideas should be the best. Let them flow, and then prioritize the best one at your discretion.

The creative servant is one who, despite his daily life, is thinking of innovating, always believing that any new idea strengthens and improves the service he provides.

Innovate because this principle will promote the way you act in the company. Guillermo Cuellar, President of Creative Awareness in Massachusetts, says, "creativity is a spark that we all have. But that spark has to be blown to grow into a flame and then fire. If you don't blow enough or don't create the atmosphere to foster the idea, it may never burn." A servant who does not let an idea run isolates himself from the company's achievements. His proposals, based on new ideas, will receive the consent of any organization.

The creative servant generates intellectual trust and respect for his projects, and the innovator earns leadership because of his business sense. Discarding an idea is not letting the desired dream flow. A positive thought is visualized triumphing in your area.

"The perfect combination to optimize professional performance and inner peace is the sum of high levels of creative passion and inner tranquility and confidence," says Santiago Alvarez de Mon, Professor of Managing People in Organizations at IESE Business School in Madrid, Spain.

The creative servant enjoys doing new things and defies the conventional. He knows his strengths, makes the most of them, and has a positive vision for creativity because he is motivated and passionate about what he does. A creative servant is persistent with what he wants, and his routine becomes a challenge to yield positive results. Franc Ponti, a business consultant, argues that "to be creative is to see things that others don't see," also that, "...people are creative at a particular time and then cease to be creative, but turn that characteristic into a habit and a way of being."

Experts say that "adults lose the children's ability to fantasize. They are so orthodox that they forget that their mind can work differently."

Creating new ideas within an organization can help you get better benefits, such as efficiency and motivation. The servant's innovation is becoming increasingly critical to business success. When the worker makes decisions for himself, he's motivated to be more creative.

Tony Buzan, the creator of mind maps and discoverer of the power of creative intelligence, assures that everything is inside the mind and that if a person traces a kind of map in his brain where ideas are not linear but free, he will feel the change. Servant, your ability to generate positive ideas builds the realization of goals for your company and the achievement of your purpose!

> *"Your first and foremost job as a leader is to take charge*
> *of your own energy and then help to orchestrate*
> *the energy of those around you."*
> **Peter Drucker**
> American-Austrian management consultant and educator

The servant with a sense of service

*"Good service is art without vanity: The vain ignores
that the artist is breathingfrom God to man."*
Emilio Galán
Chilean Philosopher

The servant with a sense of service is oblivious to dishonesty or
lack of integrity, among other detrimental behaviors; contrary
to those servants that, as a result of any of these behaviors,
do not carry out their work activity as they should, ceasing to
provide a helpful service. There is no point in being a servant
for the sake of it without knowing how to be one. A servant
with a sense of service is the one who does things right. What
keeps a servant with a sense of service alive is his work, the
desire to improve, move forward, and fight to achieve goals
vital to his company. Whoever does not find meaning in his
work will not be happy. Work, even if it unfolds at critical times
or in the worst-case scenario, is never meaningless. Handling
any vicissitude with an emotional balance allows you to move
forward and overcome any difficulties that may hinder your
intentions to work with a sense of service in the interests of
society. Experts in speech therapy argue that "between twenty
and thirty percent of people's cases of depression and anxiety
occur by subjectively believing that life is meaningless (...)."

That relates to servants working for the sake of it,
meaninglessly, without knowing why or why they are where
they work. When the worker does not find a sense of what he
does and does not seek it, he falls into gaps, confusion, and
uncertainty, which, in the end, harms him and the company
where he provides his services.

*"He who does not live to serve,
does not deserve to live."*
Mother Teresa of Calcutta
Catholic nun and missionary

Organizations should allow intellectuals and professionals to share their experiences, knowledge, and techniques to generate a better working climate.

As Greek-Egyptian poet, journalist, and civil servant Cavafy says, let us not allow life to become an unwelcome stranger. Let's do what we like. Let's love what we do. Let us draw our world, sculpt it as a work of art, being also able to see the pain of the other, to do whatever is in our power to relieve or accompany it.

Servant friend, even if you cannot experience your job the way you want, try at least/as much as possible; this allows you to grow more in your attitude as a servant with a sense of service.

Gabriel Vallejo López, a Colombian lawyer and politician, argues that "the skills required in the positions can be learned and developed, but the attitudinal ones cannot, and these are the ones that generate a real differentiation of the people in the provision of the service." Technical requirements, profession, and experience, among others, can be unknown, but the attitude of service is the main criterion. Technical skills can be learned, but the attitude of service is a vocation. A servant with a negative attitude towards the citizen injures the good name of the company. When there is no disposition to serve, the servant is absent from his true mission.

The servant with a sense of service assumes a behavior of respect for the company and, of course, the client, being careful of his servant status and accepting that humility must be part of his accomplishments.

"The greater the humility, the closer we are to greatness."
Rabindranath Tagore
Bengali poet, writer, composer, philosopher, and painter

Sincerity, the quality that enhances the servant

"Truthfulness is at the foundation of all personal excellence. It exhibits itself in conduct. It is rectitude-truth in action and shines through every word and deed."
Samuel Smiles
Scottish author and government reformer

Sincerity is vital for the optimal development of the organization; its absence significantly impairs business projects and affects the work environment. Sincerity is paramount to ensure proposals and plans; the servant who enjoys this quality gives way to quick actions for the company's benefit. On the contrary, fake, insincere kindness does not allow opinions to be shared and ideas to be discussed from all angles within the environment.

When the truth is real, it "astonishes." Truth does not pay tribute to any society, neither ancient nor modern, at the risk of living in ignorance that will lead, inevitably, to social beheading, says Emilio Galán in his work Axiological Philosophy of Law.

The character of an organization depends on how its members relate to each other and their environment. Noting how an organization talks, you can know what is and is not possible for that organization, its productivity, the business opportunities it can generate, says Rafael Echeverría.

"Lack of sincerity does not mean willful dishonesty. It means too many people don't express themselves honestly. They retain criticism to avoid conflict and sweeten bad news to keep up appearances," researchers argue.

"I fear nothing, for I keep the truth, which is powerful."
Sophocles
Greek tragedian

Not knowing how to express ideas with due sincerity injures any project that could benefit the business and the client's interests. On the contrary, the servant's sincerity allows conversations to flow positively, as ideas are discussed transparently and without prejudice.

Sincere actions and behaviors eliminate unnecessary meetings that damage productivity in the organization and therefore provide good service. Too many committees, boards, assemblies, without substantive arguments and sincerity among the member servants, make no sense and affect the transparent outcome for the benefit of the proposed organizational objectives. A sincere servant participates in active conversations where more and better ideas emerge in a natural discussion environment; any project where sincerity is not involved at all levels can be affected decisively.

Jack Welch argues: "Sincerity makes more people join the conversation. When more people participate in a talk, more ideas emerge that are discussed, dissected, and improved. Instead of everyone being silent, everyone opens up and learns." He also states that "openly shared ideas can be discussed quickly, improved and put into action."

Ramblings and misrepresentations take the meetings to an unexpected place in the absence of sincerity, which should be the protagonist or preferential guest in all work areas. The servant's sincerity awakens the trust that the client has placed in the company. The culture of letting go of the absence of sincerity should never be your ally.

Concert pianist James Rhodes states very well that "it's risky to be honest in the world today. Few people do it because it exposes us, and we may be hurt. It's easier to wear a mask and project an image of ourselves instead of reality. I've lived too long in it; I don't have the energy to keep acting. It's easier for me to talk honestly without being a fool, of course, who hurts others."

"We must not believe too much in the praise.
Criticism is sometimes much needed."
Dalai Lama
Spiritual leader of Tibetan Buddhism

The servant who does not complicate simplicity

*"What does it take to be happy? A blue sky over our heads,
a lukewarm breeze and the peace of the spirit."*
André Maurois
French author

The servant that does not complicate simplicity is the one that acts as a facilitator and provides a timely solution to the needs of the user and, in turn, provides an efficient and effective service without obstacles of any kind.

This type of servant understands the user and remains alert to detect inconveniences that may arise, listens carefully and puts himself in his exact condition, maintains a respectful, empathetic, careful, and neutral attitude towards all. He acknowledges what they tell him and repeats the key points of the interlocutor's approach to avoid misunderstandings and assure him that he is listening, asks questions if necessary, limits the discussion to the facts and what is happening in the present situation. Once the problems have been determined, he focuses on solutions.

The challenge of a servant who doesn't complicate simplicity is to turn the discussion into a solution and allow users to express their issues and opinions. The servant's ability to understand the user is a skill that enables him to address problems constructively, not as a complication. Agreements are part of this servant's work routine; they are his essence and constant challenge; the proper management of conflicts distinguishes him.

The servant who does not complicate simplicity identifies problems and disagrees with arguments, always looking for a solution. He invites the citizen to share opinions, ideas, and suggestions with an open mind without intentions to harm him but help with the means within his reach. He seeks to identify areas of concern and agreement and tries to find aspects where all can coincide, asking the customer what he lacks, what he needs, his interest, and what solutions he proposes before his goals.

This servant should be characterized by developing and practicing his facilitation skills. His ongoing challenge is to make decisions, resolve conflicts, interpret needs, identify processes that favor the community's interests, diligently attend to sensible and respectful proposals of the user.

Not complicating simplicity is to be willing to prioritize kindness as a work environment investment. The fundamental premise in this sense is to act by example based on positive attitudes and behaviors and render the service with joy, tolerance, and a sense of humor, thus enriching life, saving energy, and promoting health. The servant who does not complicate simplicity is committed to the virtue of growing in attitude; he puts the willingness to do whatever is necessary, within the ethical framework, at the forefront of his thinking to achieve his objectives. Commitment is the main feature of this servant because only those committed to an activity or a cause exclude the possibility of 'cannot' from their thinking.

The servant must observe tenacity in his ongoing effort to provide the customer with the required service without the presence of obstacles. Harmony, discipline, openness to change, optimal attention, lifelong learning, solidarity, human warmth, and speed of service are some of the fundamental skills that enable this kind of servant to provide the service that the community expects.

Remember that a servant acting on these principles is not only a guide or a counselor but a teacher every time he develops the mission to serve. Selfishness and rigidity provoke the rejection of the community. If you want to provide a good service, you must change your attitude and be more generous and understand the user's needs. Technical-professional training and expertise in one discipline or another are not sufficient to perform a task. As established, if the servant cannot relate and communicate constructively, earning the trust of society is of no use. Social skills are the whole and the essence for better institutional development.

> *"The man who makes difficult things seem easy*
> *is the educator."*
> **Ralph Waldo Emerson**
> American essayist, lecturer, philosopher, and poet

The prudent servant

> *"The best way to defend one's own secrets*
> *is respecting others."*
> **José Saramago**
> Portuguese writer

The prudent servant controls his words, avoids inappropriate terms, takes care of the scope of his expressions, and is discreet about what he may or may not say. Proper use of language allows him to dissent without assaulting the client; good sense is the fundamental element for a better understanding of the community.

For the sole fact of being a servant, you should give the best image of the company you represent, being cautious when providing information. The improper use of the word causes consequences of magnitude, damaging the good name of the entity, leading to social and often legal sanctions.

Some servants commit acts of recklessness, underestimating pronouncements by other similar companies and, often, through the media.

The servant that sees prudence as a permanent attitude takes on his business commitment with real meaning.

Talking too much and without foundation harms you in developing a better activity and hinders harmony in the organization.

Telling the truth is not an act of indiscretion, but you have to learn how it is said, at what point and without pride, so that it does not become reckless, leading to an unexpected environment.

> *"A fool's wrath is presently known:*
> *but a prudent man covereth shame."*
> **The Bible**
> Proverbs 12:16

The servant with good manners

*"Be polite; write diplomatically; even in a declaration of war, one
observes the rules of politeness."*
Otto Von Bismarck
Conservative German statesman

Good manners are fundamental to a servant's success. A servant
with optimal manners handles his behavior within the company
with appropriate habits, such as language, personal appearance, the
treatment he must have with his colleagues, and mostly the user.

Almost all bad manners occur because servants ignore what
they are doing; they are indifferent to the faults they commit. The
errors arising from these behaviors deserve immediate correction
to prevent them from transcending and producing a bad image
of the organization they represent.

It is not appropriate for a servant to take advantage of any
company celebration to drink liquor, but it is still done.

There are other inappropriate behaviors; they are
innumerable, and we would not finish enunciating them. These
behaviors should be avoided because they injure and deteriorate
the good environment that must exist in companies.
Sometimes certain servants' ego does not allow them to become
aware of the mistakes they make. They should keep in mind
that building good manners impacts better customer service
and creates an environment that encourages the culture of fair
treatment.

In terms of good manners, high-impact pamphlets
containing adequate dress codes are published in the United
States. These are instructions issued by the big companies, aimed
at their employees, to dress elegantly at the workplace. Some
servants do not accept criticism or observations about it, and
ideally, they should not act to please those who criticize them but
out of respect for themselves and the company. Certain servants
are often dressed informally at work, especially on Fridays.
Dressing well for the office maintains decorum, a sense of

dignity, and respect for the customer. Lisa Monet Agustson, an image consultant, argues that "a suit communicates discipline, maturity, style, self-respect and respect for people, with whom one meets." Today, companies that follow fashion trends point out that there is a penchant for seriousness and modesty in choosing to dress for work; curiously, young people are advocates of a good dress code.

Likewise, it is worth highlighting the employee's timely use of the cell phone or landline during his/her working hours. For example, when he prioritizes personal and unimportant calls, forcing the client to support the servant's monologue with the telephone device for a long time, not being respectful of others' time. Another act of rudeness is to enter a meeting and put the cell phone on the table; this implies an unshowy way of telling other attendees that the person will be more aware of the telephone than of them. In these cases, if an important call is being waited for, an apology should be offered before starting the meeting and retiring at the time of answering and speaking in a moderate tone, in case you cannot leave the venue.

Another relevant circumstance is the sometimes abusive use of the phone in the office.

Servant friend, the cell phone is one of the most valuable inventions today for the benefit it lends, but it should be used appropriately depending on the occasion and where you are. It is simple common sense; remember, however, that its use is expressly prohibited in some places.

Good manners transcend daily life and do not depend on social stratum. The servant that respects others by being more humane, responding with professionalism, kindness, tolerance, prudence, committed to the company and the client will always be well received. Good education cultivates 'inner elegance,' as scholars of psychology often call it.

> *"Simplicity is the ultimate sophistication."*
> **Leonardo da Vinci**
> Italian polymath and painter

The servant that manages his time

" Live as if you were to die tomorrow.
Learn as if you were to live forever".
Gandhi
Indian lawyer, anti-colonial nationalist,
and political ethicist

Time is getting shorter and shorter. It is common to hear people say: 'I don't have time'; 'there's not enough time'; 'I am busy'; 'I'll call you later.' We always live without time. Time does reach if we schedule it if we design a plan of what we have to do the day before the work activity.

'I don't have enough time,' is an expression we hear every day. That is not true. Plan it; your time will be enough. The working hours of the day become 24 if they are not scheduled. There are cases where many servants like to take work home because it gives them more time. That attitude, in a sense, is selfish because you should be productive during your working time.

Proper time management helps the servant get the most out of its use, allowing him to budget for it and efficiently fulfill projects and tasks. Although meetings consume much of the working hours, leaving very little time for other activities, it is crucial to organize and plan the utilization of available time appropriately.

A day has 24 hours, and you have to make the most of them; every hour is decisive as long as you make good use of it. A practical example of managing time in the best way is making a list of daily activities to be carried out, prioritizing essential tasks, scheduling more time for creative projects, or important ideas, especially for when you have more energy.

Time management is a challenge. Every servant should be aware of what he can achieve on a workday. When organizing the agenda, he must leave enough room for the things he must do and for the unexpected ones, minimize stress, and avoid overcommitments to himself and others.

Some servants believe that by working faster and for more hours, they will do more. However, working more quickly causes greater problems because mistakes increase; working for an extended period is exhausting, decreasing judgment and creating more inconvenience.

Stress is caused when time isn't managed well or by waiting until the last minute to run a big project. Being organized and proper planning allows you to manage time without obstacles and enjoy it as it should be, gaining health and avoiding stress.

The servant who acts according to priorities, identifying what he should and should not do with his time, can differentiate what is urgent and vital from what is important but not urgent. The first must be resolved promptly; the second can be done when there is time, specialists argue.

The servant who manages his time must make an agenda in which urgent and important matters or those that will take a long time to be completed are prioritized, taking into account complex issues and emergencies. Leaving time for the latter is of great transcendence because no matter how careful a plan is, unforeseen events always occur.

Interruptions take valuable time, especially when working on a creative project, as they can create difficulty in the resumption of the train of thought. When working on an important task, if possible, close your office door or isolate yourself from others. Time is everything for you; use it with discipline. Periodic breaks help you stay alert and focused. Keep your real agenda; if it stresses you, or you often miss your daily to-do list of activities, think again, and make the necessary adjustments.

The simulating servant

He pretends or simulates at his job, running around with papers in his hands, leaving a briefcase or purse on the desk, or the computer on when he often doesn't need it, to give the impression that he works for many hours and is always busy. Sometimes, some servants simulate reading documents related to their position, searching for information already known, or making unnecessary phone calls to pretend to be constantly busy, without proper use of the time required in the assigned mission. Use working time correctly, and shortly, you will see your fruits.

James B. Bullard, CEO and president of the Federal Reserve Bank of St. Louis, says: "Time can mean many things: money, an enemy, something that cures everything, an asset that is saved or lost; but at work, it's never on our side. Servants believe that time moves very slowly. Managers believe that it goes too fast; in general, their different perspectives illustrate the great division between bosses, who tend to believe that being present amounts to productivity and employees who often feel compelled to show signs of commitment to the company." A well-used time pays homage to your work effectiveness.

The loyal servant

"Don't you have enemies?
Have you never told the truth or never loved justice?"
Santiago Ramón y Cajal
Spanish neuroscientist and Nobel laureate

Loyalty is the value of values for a servant. A loyal servant is faithful to the postulates of the company, looks at it with respect, responsibility, honesty, and commitment. A servant with principles is a loyal servant. The most profound commitment is his institution. It is also the result of the correct performance. Servant loyalty must be vital to maintaining the trust of the organization.

Loyalty is a virtue that guarantees the work environment. Reservation and prudence enhance the principles of companies, the essence of the true servant. From a loyal servant, the best and unconditional work for his company is expected.

The loyal servant provides confidence and security to his superior. For him, it is bleak to be disappointed by his collaborators.

As a boss, how would you feel if your trusted assistant intends your position or uses obscure strategies to hurt you? Or, quite the opposite, when a superior uses the same procedures with his immediate collaborators, requesting the transfer or disengagement, for simple convenience.

The essence of his mission as a servant is the commitment to a cause: the institution. It is then when his value carries him perennial in time and does not make his worst enemy from whoever his boss has been. He is the one who pays tribute to gratitude; he is transparent in his proceeding with his superiors, colleagues, and, fundamentally, with the entity. He is honest with himself making himself a full servant.

> *"Friendship can only take place through the development of mutual respect and in a spirit of sincerity."*
> ***Dalai Lama***
> Spiritual leader of Tibetan Buddhism

Wherever fraud, deception, or betrayal are, homage is paid to corruption.

Say NO to the presence of these anti-values, which destroy business interests and your detriment as a human being, says writer Pilar Velez.

> *"Envy is a thousand times worse than hunger, since it is hunger of the spirit."*
> ***Miguel de Unamuno***
> Spanish essayist, philosopher, and writer

The visionary servant

The visionary servant seeks the permanent change of processes in strategic planning, new forms of motivation, and the creation of procedures. These are "different employees" in generating new tools and strategies to ensure a better service.

Thanks to new techniques, organizations have found innovative formulas that channel them into better customer service. A visionary servant focuses on developing ideas or procedures that no one else has in mind and anticipates proposals, becoming a pioneer of his environment. He is the one who brings dynamics to the organization and breaks with conventional models by establishing new schemes that favor the correct organizational climate.

With the rapid advancement of knowledge, increasingly fast-paced, the new systems used by organizations require the visionary servant to stay up-to-date and acquire new competencies for better job performance. The visionary servant that improves work skills adds to the institution, as he meets the customer's expectations. In this age, the servant must excel and ascend into knowledge. Seeking to go further and be one step ahead in the demands of society favors the provision of a better service.

When the servant deepens his knowledge, the change in the organization is evident and positively impacts it. The most knowledgeable visionary servant acquires more skills that impact his professional growth and affect the institution's success.

The visionary servant is not intimidated by difficult situations; he has fast, consistent and practical solutions. He makes his thoughts come true, advances executions that no one is doing, solidifies his ideas departing from the usual and ordinary, breaking with an established model that, in most cases, does not allow the organization to grow. The visionary servant breaks the schematics and is daring in positioning the company productively. For a servant with projection, novelty is its challenge; he is the one who causes positive changes with a proactive attitude.

The visionary servant puts an end to the traditionally worn paradigms to generate a different dynamic and achieve the desired goals. He takes on unusual challenges, faces risks, and is not afraid of failure; he is a 'true servant with projection.'

> *"Constantly preparing is valuing overcoming."*
> **Miguel Angel Cornejo**
> Mexican author

The nonconformist servant

The nonconformist servant is not satisfied with his employment because he does not like the activity he develops, he did not find an opportunity to practice his profession, he does not agree with the boss or the company's policies, or his relationships with his peers or the salary are not the best. He sees his position more as an enemy than as a benefit. The critical part is that these people do not express their discontent but keep it a secret, which generates resentment.

To avoid falling into the previous state, it is recommended to handle situations with balance, keeping resentments that may be counterproductive to internal health and projected to others. Criticism should be adopted as the best ally, with simplicity, and it will improve the level of performance. Discontent can lead to low activity development, harming both colleagues and users.

> *"Anything that helps you feel better will always attract more of the same."*
> **John Gray**
> American counselor

The change in attitude is favorable if frustrations are left aside and if one has the sense to build cooperation between colleagues. That will make a better journey to change for the benefit of oneself and the company. A rigid position leads to nothing; it is essential to close circles and prepare to open new ones, which will provide a better work experience.

CHAPTER IV

Leadership and entrepreneurship on the servant

Liderazgo en el servidor

"Good leadership means leading others and even advocating guidelines from others without attacking freedom."
Victor Frankl
Austrian psychiatrist

The most important aspect that a servant must consider to be a good leader is the will to be one or the desire to become one. In reality, few servants recognize the enormous value the will has on their achievement; without it, nothing gets started, and the goal is not reached. A servant can have many skills in his favor: talent, experience, transparency, honesty, sympathy, etc. but if he does not have the desire or willingness to become a good leader and does not do what is necessary to achieve it, he will never be able to fulfill his goal or transform the reality in which he lives. A challenge must be present to lead any organization, making it the best ally to achieve the proposed objectives.

What are the qualities of a great leader? Without a doubt, knowledge, intelligence, and vision. Add to this emotional intelligence, defined as the ability to identify and monitor emotions, both own and those of others, to manage interpersonal relationships.

Features associated with emotionally intelligent people:

1. **They are self-aware**: realistic self-confidence. They know well what their strengths and weaknesses are; they operate according to their competencies and know when to rely on other team members.
2. **They have emotional acumen**: they understand their own emotions. That, for example, allows them to

> know what angers them; it helps them control anger.
3. **They exercise self-control. Resilience**: they keep calm under pressure and recover quickly from disappointments. They are not victims of panic. During crises, they seek comfort in the leader. If they see him calm, they calm down.
4. **They have emotional balance**, keeping distressing feelings under control. Instead of getting mad at people, they explain the problem and offer them a solution.
5. **They motivate themselves** without losing sight of the goals despite the setbacks.
6. **They feel cognitive and emotional empathy**: they understand different perspectives than their own and present things in a way that others understand them. They also encourage others to ask questions to make sure they understand what has been explained to them. Cognitive empathy, along with the ability to accurately interpret the feelings of others, is the key to effective communication.
7. **They know how to listen**, trying their best to understand what the other person is saying without interrupting them or imposing their own agenda.
8. **They know how to relate to others**, expressing their views clearly and persuasively by motivating people and clearly explaining what is expected.
9. **They work as a team**, making others feel at ease in their presence. Proof of this is that they laugh easily, author and science journalist Daniel Goleman argues.

In an increasingly virtual world, skills for human relationships and leadership have been lost. Today we need a leader who motivates and inspires others while promoting traditional leadership attributes. The current crisis in this regard is primarily due to the incredible technological revolution we are experiencing; there is a worldwide leadership gap in all our most important institutions: government, business, education, religion, art, etc.

Bosses should be aware that their roles are becoming more public, as social media and constant electronic communications expose issues that were once kept behind closed doors. It is then when prudence plays a key role.

Gustavo Mutis, a leadership and strategic management consultant, says that "the true leader does not seek his own leadership. Instead, he seeks to remove dependencies and bindings. That's where the greatness of his mission lies."

One of the leader's first goals is aspiring to win the goodwill and support of those who are part of his organization. A servant unable to help his collaborators grow and rise above their daily life will not become a good leader since he will not be aware of the need to offer himself to form other leaders within his organization.

A leading servant may have a vision for the future, but his momentum has no reason to be if he has no virtue. The best compass of those who wish to become exemplary leaders is clarity in their competencies, the organization, and their own planning. A leader who raises awareness and gains support is the ultimate leader because he does not see others below him. His attitude opposes the imposition of authoritarianism, which is often the cause of a departure from the sense of good leadership.

Arthur Shirk, founder of Coaching Hall International and leadership expert, says that "it's not just about knowing more, because leaders already know what skills they need, the key is to see what things about their personality prevents them from developing skills."

A leader does not just need to develop critical service skills and competencies; he should also complement his training as a human being. His emotional stability allows him to be aware of what is going on around him.

> *"When pride comes, disgrace will follow,*
> *but with humility comes wisdom."*
> **The Bible**
> Proverbs 11:2

Knowing how to listen can be one of his most essential skills since a listening servant with a sense of leadership gains accurate information, identifies and clarifies problems creatively, and makes substantive decisions to resolve conflicts seamlessly. A leader with a sense of listening knows what is going on within his business or organization. When he listens carefully to his team and the community, he learns to be better. Elaine Biech, an international consultant, argues that "you always have to listen in all directions of the organization because, from the base level, your perception can be an opinion for change."

Listening plays a vital role in building harmonic teams; hence a good connection with the members will show interest in them and their work. The best suggestion is to have an open mind and avoid presumptions and judgments. A study with outstanding people in different fields highlights these qualities:

- Dreaming: they rely on ideals, think big, and dare to transform reality.
- Passion: they give themselves with love to a mission, and that love gives them the strength to persist without surrendering.
- Sensitivity: They shine for their service capacity, their human sense, and their solidarity.
- Curiosity: they love to explore, ask questions, and live open to amazement.
- Preparation: they live by learning, and they do not stop studying and training.
- Good humor and resilience: They focus on the positive and do not lose heart in the face of adversity and challenges; it is as if they enjoy overcoming obstacles.

Developing these skills allows the leader to realize his goals. For ManpowerGroup president Jeff Joerres, who participated in the 2012 Davos Economic Forum for the "Human Age," or when the scarce good that gives value to the economy is human talent since capital, resources, and technology are nothing if there are no people. He also argues that a "leadership that privileges the human is what will make societies and their economies sustainable. The "Human Age" is the true essence of organizations."

"Leadership is no longer exercised with power,
now it has to do alsowith inspiring influence
and building coalitions and alliances."
Francisco Thiermann
CEO of IBM Chile

Leadership is a popular topic today. The world is complex, changing, and all organizations need leaders who influence others to meet goals and challenges, leading others into the future with a purpose and confidence.

Within his eight leadership rules, Jack Welch says that "leaders are constantly improving their team, using each encounter as an opportunity to evaluate, advise, and create self-confidence." It is about knowing how to advise your collaborators, guiding them towards the best performance in all its aspects. A leading servant who does not drive self-confidence wastes energy and affects the sense of vision that his employees may have; this security promotes a positive vision for the future. The leader who transmits it fosters an environment of optimism and overcoming continuous challenges in his team. A leader with these characteristics gives credence to his people, even in turbulent times.

A servant that projects himself with constant vision and confidence transmits life and encourages new challenges. A leader must demonstrate an energetic attitude to overcome difficult moments in the organization; a good sense of humor is contagious and opens up confidence for good job development.

What makes a leader? There are some studies and research on the subject expressing different opinions. Summing up, some of the qualities that characterize a leader with a sense of service are organization, motivation, a vision of the future, audacity to take risks, passion, courage, inspiration, fearlessness, continuous training, critical thinking, and good direction in their social skills. A servant leader must raise the levels of the predictable in understanding, control, and compassion for his people.

If a leader intends to lead an organization and get it excited, he must necessarily have moral integrity, good feelings, and positive attitudes that make sense of his virtue to become what society expects of him. Also, a true leader does pedagogy with his attitudes; he is an example to imitate.

Many bosses suffer from power poisoning and believe they are aware of every significant development in the organization, even when they cannot hide the fact that they entirely ignore critical issues. According to Robert I. Suston, professor of management science at the Stanford University School of Engineering, this is known as 'the fallacy of centrality,' where the leader assumes to know everything and what it takes to execute effective leadership by enjoying a central position. Leadership, however, was not based on these characteristics but other aspects, as L. Kevin Kelly, former Chief Executive Officer of Heidrick & Struggles, clearly states: "The value of leadership lies in making decisions that are for the benefit of the organization above oneself."

"The art of directing people requires the manager to be willing to help his employees develop their professional skills and abilities, but also to achieve success in personal and family life," experts argue.

Why do servants fail?

The answer to this question is simple; servants fail because they make serious errors in the performance of their functions, which can cause them to fall into the abyss.

First of all, they do not innovate enough, and since there is a lack of creativity, it is impossible that even though they are intelligent, they can achieve good results. The quality and speed of the changes they make are below what circumstances demand. Many professional servants fall asleep on their laurels. They think they have already discovered the permanent formula of success. They are not friends of innovations that are not the product of their imagination because they believe that no one better than them can detect what changes need to be made.

They also misinterpret reality; they are wrong in the visions they define for the entity or company and are very efficient in making that misconception a reality. 'Executive' servants, as their name suggests, are very good at executing but are not necessarily adept at defining the great institutional dream they want to achieve. Unique talents are required to not deviate from the intended objectives due to the desire to achieve results. Understanding the environment is a very complex task. It requires many hours of learning and studying economic, political, and social aspects, which are necessary, but that bore or confuse many.

> *"He who has faith in himself does not need others believe in it."*
> **Miguel de Unamuno**
> Spanish essayist, philosopher

CAPÍTULO V

The servant's ethics and values

*"Always prefer poverty without fault
to ill-acquired riches."*

Aristotle
Greek philosopher

Other fundamental characteristics of the servant must be tolerance, sensitivity, and responsibility, which allow him to become aware of the situation of others, accepting the pressures and frustrations that arise in the environment, which leads to an increase in capacity and a better attitude in their environment.

Within the above characteristics, we must welcome those values that provide us with a better path, such as those that guide and serve life, dignifying the person, integrating it better into society, developing to the maximum the qualities that finally perfect it and allow it to become a better servant.

Ethical values of the good servant

Values are rules of conduct or qualities of individuals, considered in this case as desirable for the fulfillment of the mission that corresponds to the servant.

Among the fundamental values and principles of the servant are the following:

- Respect for others
- Loyalty
- Commitment
- Teamwork

- Professionalism
- Participation
- Responsibility
- Transparency in stocks
- Quality
- Productivity
- Compliance

1. Respect for others.

The good servant should treat other people with respect, the same way he would like to be treated. Always find the positive points of the people you deal with daily and adopt a habit of focusing on those positive points. Always express respect to your superiors and companions, giving them courteous and attentive treatment. Carry out the same attitude when serving customers in fulfillment of your mission.

2. Loyalty.

Encouraging loyalty to the organization is a fundamental rule of conduct on every excellent servant. Loyalty contributes to consolidating the ethical values of those who serve the State or any institution.

3. Commitment.

Commitment means giving yourself entirely to the fulfillment of business goals. Commitment is generated by itself and is based on each servant's intimate convictions. Make a list of commitments you have each day with your work and your institution and check it daily to ensure the degree of fulfillment of each obligation. Remember that every good servant is a person committed to his company and that the lack of commitment leads inevitably to failure.

4. Teamwork.

Working together is one of the values of every good servant. Teamwork demands the loyalty and commitment of the group members. Teamworking servants perform their tasks in harmony, support each other, and identify with their institution's goals. Within the team, the members use their strengths to counter the weaknesses of others. Pay attention to your team's operation and their participation in it. Remember that if your work together is good, you are a good servant.

5. Professionalism.
The vocation of service leads to the professional judgment of the worker. Fulfilling your position or job activities with professionalism means acting with opportunity, quality, economy, and efficiency. That is, complying with the principles of administrative action.

6. Participation.
Participation is key to commitment and democracy in the workplace. It has a lot to do with the sense of belonging to the institution in which one works. Participating and sharing is a two-way process of self-giving.

7. Responsibility.
Being responsible implies assuming the consequences of the actions that each servant executes and those derived from them. As a good servant, spend a portion of your time determining your levels of responsibility.

8. Transparency in actions.
Each servant's actions must be exemplary. That means that a servant's actions must be crystal clear and cannot generate any doubt.

9. Quality.
The servant must stand out for his personal and professional qualities. In fulfilling his mission, he will need to seek that the seal of superiority is imposed in his work, always to make it competitive, and contribute to fulfilling organizational objectives. As an immediate goal, propose to carry out your tasks with quality.

10. Productivity.

The good servant should aim to perform as many relevant tasks or actions in the shortest possible time, with the lowest costs and the best quality.

Compliance. Compliance is another fundamental value of every good servant. Therefore, maintain that line of action. Be rigorous in fulfilling your activities and commitments, and immediately fulfill what you promised if you forgot to do so. If you are the boss and keep your promises, your collaborators will follow suit.

The servant's behavior

"There are many things in life more important than money.
But they cost so much money!"
Groucho Marx
American comedian, actor, writer, and television star

The servant's conduct is part of the principles and rules that make up an ethical culture. The servant's behavior must be driven by honesty, which translates into righteousness and honesty at work. Likewise, service efficiency must permanently characterize the conduct of the person exercising the function.

The principles of accountability, transparency, and impartiality must also be part of this conduct. Generally speaking, the servant must observe a neat conduct in his actions to benefit the collective interest

Corruption

" Put a rogue in the limelight, and he will
act like an honest man."
Napoleon Bonaparte
French statesman, military leader, and Emperor of *France*

Corruption is an act for the personal benefit or that of third parties, contrary to fundamental values, which violates the interest of the user and the common welfare. Codes of ethics are never part of the corrupt, violating the legal system, harming free competition, causing social harm and poverty, concentrating income, increasing costs, affecting the business climate, breaking the order, damaging the image, and growing inequality. This universal scourge is the worst mole of any society.

"Every servant is the owner of his actions
and a slave to their consequences."
Jesús Neira Quintero

CHAPTER VI

Taking care of your emotional health

The servant with emotional illness

"Being emotionally honest
is to be more real and authentic, to respect yourself,
which is a prerequisite for considering
and respect others."

Robert K. Cooper
Scholar and leadership adviser

The servants that do not handle their emotions inside the company create an unsustainable work environment. These servants often behave with attitudes of resentment, neurosis, isolation, distraction, and nostalgia. Their lack of growth infects the environment and decreases productivity.

On certain occasions, they become emotionally illiterate, not accepting any recommendations from their superior and less from their peers. The servant that is willing to direct his emotional states builds a better business morning.

"Regulate your emotions and learn how to handle them. Understand the emotions of others to forgive the mistakes of others or avoid making those mistakes and learn to handle feelings in a way that doesn't affect anyone, not even you," Daniel Goleman says.

Compassion, patience, and self-awareness make people leaders and team members. If a servant lacks these elements, the company is likely to face misfortune.

When servants use their emotional intelligence well, they contribute to creating an emotionally intelligent enterprise. The quality of the organization is up to you.

Anxiety and the servant

"It is not to have received a lesson that saves us,
but to have been able to take advantage of it."
George Canning
British Tory statesman

Anxiety in the worker can affect the mood to carry out their work better, as excessive worry does not allow them to perform activities properly.

When the servant is very anxious, he cannot concentrate, even though he has a schedule. If the worker feels anxiety, he reacts desperately and, in the face of circumstances, even eliminates his creativity, which prevents him from getting better performance in the proposed task. This emotional disorder affects the environment and makes it difficult to tune in with your work.

Having a high level of anxiety causes cognitive and emotional disturbances, affecting behavior or willingness to work. Therefore, an adjustment of interpersonal skills facilitates the construction of the well-being of the company itself.

Excessive anxiety affects projects and harms people's willingness. Workers with high levels of anxiety must be continuously trained not only in aspects such as their job development but also on significant issues such as stress management, as this will result in better performance.

It is important to note that a state of anxiety "occurs only in situations where something is at stake, a result that you are interested in, that can be good or bad or with the threat of an unwanted result," explains Antonio Cano Vindel, president of the Spanish Society for the Study of Anxiety and Stress.
According to the study Anxiety Disorders, conducted by Jaime Vila Castellar and Gustavo Reyes del Paso, professors of the Universities of Granada and Jaén, "anxiety can be a mental disorder whose most important symptom is the excessive or chronic concern that may be generated in work environments."

That does not mean that the solution to anxiety episodes is the loss of the worker's sense of responsibility in the face of his position. Still, when the concern is a consequence of not having organized work-related points, it is evident that this phenomenon occurs.

How to avoid work anxiety?

"Stop, breathe, reflect and choose," the experts say. Make the best decision after exhausting these steps. Above all, keep in mind that the best choice is made at rest, not to make mistakes that will later affect your health and vital interpersonal relationships for your performance.

Welcome! The four elements mentioned are the basis for learning to manage anxiety when difficulties arise in your work.

Plan your time and be a better worker based on the intelligent handling of the items of your competence. It's all in the attitude. It is possible to control that feeling of helplessness when anxiety wants to take advantage. Master your reactions, focus on staying relaxed; it is all about will in the face of your emotions.

Anxiety affects the worker's morale, leads to moodiness, excessive worry, and lack of concentration. That is why you must become aware of your condition and keep your balance. Be assertive to understand these kinds of behaviors better; try to focus on positive thoughts and lift your energy. Stress, a consequence of your anxiety, is not the best ally. Reflect on which values move you, do not stray from the marked path to not lose your brand because anxiety significantly affects its surroundings and leads to the deterioration of your image. Highlight your strengths and neutralize weak areas to avoid incidents that affect you.

The best recommendation in these cases is to be aware of your feelings and emotions, both positive and negative, of your ability to choose and manage the situation in an appropriate and timely manner. Consider the consequences of getting carried away by anxiety impulses. Direct your thoughts toward what you are going to achieve. Focus entirely on the result and choose the right emotion; emotions depend on your perspective.

It is increasingly common to find workers concerned for no apparent reason, reacting very quickly to the most diverse situations, easily altered, do many things simultaneously and in a messy way, maintaining an accelerated pace, and finding it difficult to relax.

Many suffer from anxiety attacks, that state of restlessness, that diffuse feeling of anguish that opens the door for the person to become conflicted and not perform their role. In these cases, the worker should become self-aware and gain self-control, one of the most important emotional intelligence skills, as it involves the development of a series of alternative actions to replace and avoid excessive reactions.

If the worker turns anxiety into a routine, the time will come when all circuits are altered and collapse on the job site. To avoid this, every servant must see problems as challenges and seek solutions. That will give you well-being and peace of mind. In other words, you must see anxiety as a challenge.

"Get rid of anxiety about the things of this world;
don't let yourself be governed by the illusions
of this perishable world."
Bhagavad Gita
Hindu scripture

One of the qualities that allow maintaining serenity in the daily situations related to the provision of service is impartiality, hence the importance of the worker keeping it. The servant that reaches this state in his consciousness sees his responsibility unaffected. The person who maintains serenity in both success and adversity makes the best decisions.

A good worker does not expect rewards derived from the service provided; he is only concerned with the correct fulfillment of his duties. This perspective does not allow anxiety to take control and provides calm permanently because the only concern of the good servant will be fulfilling his obligations.

Study, research, and discover the areas related to your work, especially those where the most problems arise, to find the result you want to reach. That prevents stress from worsening your anxiety level and achieve fulfillment.

Remember this tip from French pharmacist and psychologist Emile Coué: "Every day, in every way, I'm getting better and better." The above is a deep reflection to consider when you do things as they should be.

In the meantime, we present a basic concept for reducing anxiety. Resilience is "a special skill that successfully overcomes traumatic life situations," argue researchers from the American Psychological Association. It is also "the process of adapting well to adversity, trauma, tragedy, threats or even to significant sources of stress." Concerning anxiety, Professor Robert Nitsch of the Institute for Translational Neuroscience in Germany states that: "[...] at the base of resilience there is a function of the brain, but it also depends on social structures, workspace, and social relations."

Resilience allows the worker to overcome difficulties. It is a suitable means of achieving the necessary rest and not reinforcing the anxiety that affects work and creates a social and emotional disorder responsible for lack of missionary development. Beat adversity and don't let it take advantage in complex situations so that anxiety is not what ends up deciding and leading you down undesirable paths. Every time you misinterpret what you don't want for your life, you enter the realm of fear.

If you do not correctly guide your organization's expectations or goals, you will be exposed to a situation of anxiety and often insecurity. That is why it is convenient to know the origin of the problems and identify the reality to take charge and better manage emotions. That is a benchmark of your job success.

It is best to go to tranquility because it will give way to overcoming the situation. It is essential that workers feel good as human beings so that their work is fruitful. As a recommendation, practice, and exercise in approaching peers related to your interests. That will allow you to access the right emotions.

How to manage stress?

Despite the advancement of technology, making it easier to perform better at work, today's servant is more stressed because he allows his Self to take advantage, not setting priorities that affect his reality despite having the logistics necessary to carry out his functions.

Work stress should be avoided by establishing what is essential and what to expect. According to cognitive tests and at work by researchers and psychologists, learning to identify and manage stress reactions allows you to live healthier and improve performance.

The universe is governed by laws of order and precision, in everything big and small. However, some servants adopt improvisation as a formula for solving routine. American psychologists Robert Sharpe and David Lewis point out that "every mental and physical health phenomenon is within you, and it is up to you to decide how it reacts to external life situations. So educate your senses." Avoid external situations from harming work activity and identify factors that cause discomfort. Before you worry, ponder whether it is worth letting external situations affect health and activity.

"Freedom is the proper human capacity
to self-control."
Viktor Frankl
Austrian psychiatrist and philosopher

Work stress is also caused by work addiction; your attitude, in this case, does not necessarily mean greater productivity. You should not be against the servant that performs his functions thoroughly.

Still, it is necessary to distinguish between the responsible and the addict because the latter is often absent from his family, creating instability in the home, which will undoubtedly affect work performance.

There is already legal regulation in Japan concerning overwork. Experts point out that karoshi, the Japanese word meaning overwork death, would claim the lives of 10,000 Japanese each year. The desire for excellence and unlimited competence is the cause of social illness generated by work stress! Think about it!

> *" The cynic knows the price of everything*
> *and the value of nothing."*
> **Oscar Wilde**
> Irish poet and playwright

Excessive work produces stress, evident in those servants of strong temperament, who cannot avoid being as they are and end up in rigid attitudes, succumbing to panic or anger when things do not go well, polluting and transmitting their stress onto others.

Marathon days and improper time management are stealing the servant's peace of mind; productivity increases in the technical aspect but calm decreases, causing stress. The servant that manages his work stresses analyzes complex problems, suggests solutions, opens spaces that invite reflection, and generates opinion. Being dedicated, transparent, whole, recognizing mistakes, asking for help and advice, listening to others, having a good sense of humor, and meditating serenely to solve problems, gives you balance.

Work stress leads to social depression. Managing stress is recreating our relationships to optimize them even if this is not easy, but personal and work development will be harmed if it is not done.

According to a study published in the Journal of Occupational and Environmental Medicine and written by Elizabeth Kleppa of the University of Bergen, Norway, "prolonged working hours cause stress, raising the risk of disease and injury." The study also showed that working for extended hours is associated with anxiety and depression in both men and women.

"Managing emotions can help you in your career."
Kris Maher
Journalist

The work stress that overwhelms the servant is the one that has a relation to the person because there is no orderly agenda within each one of us, and no strategies that favor the Self are used. It is important to set priorities, do things at your own pace, take a moment a day to relax, and learn to say no. Understand the situations or circumstances of others, making sure you do not take the stress of others as your own. It is necessary not to be infected with external factors.

Claudia Marcela Mutis, Training Manager of the Leadership and Management Center in Colombia, argues that "work stress is conceptualized as the set of phenomena that occur in the worker's body with the participation of harmful stressors that, derived directly from or due to work, affect the worker's health."

She also adds, "work stress is the result of an imbalance between the demands that come from work and the work environment and our resources to cope. When there is too much or a constant mismatch between what work and the working environment demand and the ability to respond, a state of physical and psychological tension appears relating to a multitude of problems for the worker and the organization in which he performs his work."

Accelerated changes in procedures consequently affect servants in their work routines, thereby changing the work environment and increasing stress. That is where we must minimize the style of work, reflecting on active participation, organization, administration, and a good direction in human relations to generate a working environment with a better quality of business life.

"When an organization stresses, its performance deteriorates," experts say.

When servants manage to find meaning in what they do or the activity they develop, they are more stress-resistant.

Stress hurts the organization falling into poor performance and affecting the quality of service. One way to avoid stress is for the organization to give the servant autonomy and develop his decision-making capacity without abusing it and supporting its projects.

The entity must be fair in the tasks assigned not to fall into the irrational increase in workload to avoid the consequences of work stress.

How to create a work stress-free company?

Studies indicate that despite the difficulty involved, a company can seek improvement in the health and satisfaction of its employees and optimize its performance through the search for excellence in the organization of work and the management of human assets. Some of the golden rules for creating a work stress-free company include:

- Ensure respect for the dignity of each employee.
- Ensure that job responsibility is in line with the worker's ability.
- Give content to the job.
- Clearly define the roles and responsibilities of the worker.
- Improve communication.
- Facilitate work-life balance.

"God did not condemn man to work, but to live, granting him work as a mitigating circumstance."
Lagoreve

Balance must be maintained in all orders. One possibility is to aspire to be happy, have abundance, harmony, and achieve an integral development, with balance and goodwill, without getting carried away by stress, a silent enemy, which can end with a project of life and work development.

A self-critical, flexible, cheerful, energetic, creative spirit, combined with art, music, and intelligent humor, helps combat stress. That provides a more harmonious and balanced environment.

As human beings, we are participants or spectators of interpersonal conflicts. Whatever the area of conflict, the magnitude it reaches, the number and type of involved, conflict is an industry in full development, an industry that generates stress. While this is a reality, conflicts are neither good nor bad; the outcome will depend on how they are handled. From this perspective, it is vitally important to know and experience a systematic process for conflicts that enhances its advantages.

> *"Without the guidance of the passions,*
> *reasoning has neither principles nor power."*
> **Robert C. Solomon**
> American professor of philosophy

The servant and his emotional quotient

"Success is all about going from failure to failure
without losing enthusiasm."
Winston Churchill
Former Prime Minister of the United Kingdom

"By developing the emotional quotient is how we learn to easily recognize and value the basic sensations in ourselves and others and appropriately respond to them. Recognizing that emotions provide vital and potentially beneficial information every minute of the day (...)." If the servant handles his emotional quotient correctly, he will avoid making mistakes. To this end, he should find support on the following pillars:

- Emotional attitude. It shapes the authenticity, credibility, and flexibility of the individual, expanding his circle of trust and ability to listen, managing conflicts, and making the most of constructive discontent.
- Emotional Depth. One explores ways to shape his life and work with his unique potential and the purpose of supporting this with integrity, commitment, and responsibility, which in turn increases his influence without authority.
- Emotional alchemy. By which you will extend your creative instinct and ability to flow with problems and pressures and to compete with the future by building your capabilities to perceive and have access to hidden solutions and new opportunities.

"Intelligence is not to make no mistakes, but quickly to
see how to make them good."
Bartolt Brecht
German theatre practitioner, playwright, and poet

Bibliography

- **Abbot Arango,** *Darius. Basic steering elements.* Legis Editores S.A., 1991.
- **Armstron, Michael.** *Human Resources Management.* Legis Editores S.A. 1993.
- **Chiavenato, Idalberto, et al.** *Administración De Recursos Humanos.* McGraw-Hill, 1996.
- **Conference «The art of leadership in an age of new challenges,» Heifetz Ronald,** *Leadership and Management Center,* Bogota, February 2008.
- **Cooper, Robert K, and Ayman Sawaf.** *Emotional intelligence.* Bogotá, Editorial Norma S.A.1998.
- **Vienna Declaration and Programme of Action,** 14-25 June 1993.
- **The Spectator.** Bogota, 2003-2005
- **Goleman, Daniel.** *Destructive Emotions.* Bloomsbury, 2004.
- **Goleman, Daniel.** *Emotional Intelligence: Why it can matter more tan IQ.* Bantam, 2005.
- **Goleman, Daniel.** *Social Intelligence: The New Science of Human Relationships.* Bantam, 2007.
- **Hill, Napoleon.** *Success Through Positive Mental Attitude.* HarperCollins Pub Ltd, 1997.
- **Ibanez, Gustavo.** Bogota. 1999.
- **Lama Dalai,** *Conversations with the Dalai Lama,* Editorial Planeta Colombiana S.A., Bogotá 2006.
- **Memories, Great Leadership and Public Management Forum,** *Leadership and Management Center (CLG),* Bogota February 19 and 20, 2008.
- *Uniform Rules on Equal Opportunities for Persons with Disabilities,* Resolution 48/96 of 20 December 1993.
- **Ojeda Awad, Alonso.** *Cohabitation and Globalization Contributions for Peace,* Editorial Universidad Pedagogical Nacional, Bogotá, 2002
- **Pabón, Pedro Alfonso.** *Crimes against the public administration.* **Edit.** Science and Law. 1997.
- **Paramés Montenegro, Carlos.** *Introducción al Management.* Instituto Nacional de la Administración Pública. Madrid 1988.
- **Newspaper** *El Tiempo,* The Book of Coexistence, July 3, 2003.
- **Newspaper** *El Tiempo,* Revista Carrusel No. 1233 of July 4, 2003.

- **Newspaper** *Triumphs,* «For those who seek excellence,» Examples 2008.
- **Hoffmann, Spencer.** *Los 15 Milagros del Amor.* HarperCollins Español, 2015.
- **Pino Ricci, Jorge, et al,** *Regimen de Contratación Estatal.* Universidad Externado de Colombia, 1996.
- **Portfolio, Friday, October 3,** 2003. 2016, 2017.
- **Revista** *El Espectador,* July6, 2003, by María Antonieta Solórzano.
- **Magazine,** *The Challenge, The Environment, Air Pollution,* July-August 2004.
- **Magazine,** *Living Planet to the Limit,* Environmental Markets,2008.
- **Savater, Fernando,** *El Valor de Educar.* Editorial Ariel S.A., 1997
- **Thompson, Philip C.,** *Quality circles: How to Make Them Work in America.* AMACOM, 1982.
- **Waterman, Robert, et al.** *In Search of Excellence: Lessons from America's Best-Run Companies.* HarperTrade, 1982
- **Galán, Emilio.** *Axiological Philosophy of Law.* La Editorial, Miami Florida USA 2013.
- **Goleman, Daniel.** *Primal Leadership: Unleashing The Power of Emotional Intelligence.* Harvard Business Review Press, 2013
- **Innova,** *Newsletter of the Institute of Studies of the Public Ministry.*
- **Executive Summary,** *Analysis of the different factors that allow contributions from the solidarity economy to an agenda for peaceful coexistence in Colombian society.*
- *Culture of Legality and Integrity for Colombia, Attorney General of the Nation.* Institute of Public Ministry Studies.

About the Author

Jesus Neira Quintero is a Colombian lawyer, professor, lecturer, and writer. He has received national and international recognition for his work and commitment to education and culture. He is the author of *El Buen Servidor Público*, required textbook in different universities, seminars, and symposia; *El Arte de Servir con Felicidad*, prizewinner in the International Latino Books Award; and Servir con Humanidad. Among his many participations as a speaker and exhibitor are: XII International Meeting of Women Writers Marjory Stoneman Douglas, held at Florida International University (Miami, September 2016). Ulibro - UNAB (Bucaramanga, August 2016). United Latin American Foundation (Doral, Florida, April 2016). Congress USA (Washington, 2015). V International Congress of State Procurement and Public Budget - Instituto de Estudios del Ministerio Público (Bogotá, 2015). Colombia Summit in Washington (2014). IV Congress for the Formation of Military Leaders respectful and guarantors of Human Rights and International Humanitarian Law - Military Forces of Colombia (Bogotá, 2010). AARCO (Mexico City, April 2015). Consulate of Colombia in Mexico City (April 2015). Philanthropic Foundations (Washington, June 2009) and at the World Summit - Colombian American Chamber of Commerce Washington (December 2008).

Jesus Neira Quintero was awarded the International Prize for Literature, "Latinos en el Exterior" in recognition of the book *El Buen Servidor Público* (Washington, June 2009). He serves as a Goodwill Ambassador for the Hispanic Heritage Literature Organization/Milibrohispano.org.

Recently the Colombian Society of Press and Communication conferred on him the Order of Law and Democracy Francisco de Paula Santander for his professional and social career.

www.jesushneira.com

www.ingramcontent.com/pod-product-compliance
Lightning Source LLC
LaVergne TN
LVHW041323080426
835513LV00008B/564